FOOLISH DICK.

RICHARD HAMPTON.

FOOLISH DICK:

An Autobiography

OF

RICHARD HAMPTON,

The Cornish Pilgrim Preacher.

WITH INTRODUCTION AND NOTES.

BY

S. W. CHRISTOPHERS,

Author of "Hymn Writers and their Hymns," "Homes of old English Writers," &c.

LONDON·
HAUGHTON & CO., 10, PATERNOSTER ROW.

CONTENTS.

	PAGE
PREFACE	vii

CHAPTER I.

DICK'S FAMILY LINE AND FIRST APPEARANCE IN THE
 WORLD 9

CHAPTER II.

DICK'S EARLY DAYS OF LABOUR, SORROW, AND JOY . 25

CHAPTER III.

DICK'S INTRODUCTION TO PUBLIC LIFE 41

CHAPTER IV.

DICK'S FIRST MOVEMENT OVER THE BORDER . . . 57

CHAPTER V.

DICK'S ITINERANCY IN DEVONSHIRE 71

CHAPTER VI.

	PAGE
Dick's Perambulations among his own Kindred	88

CHAPTER VII.

Dick's Last Ramble on Tamar Side 102

CHAPTER VIII.

Recollections of Dick in his Later Life . . 119

CHAPTER IX.

The Last Days of Dick's Pilgrimage . . . 134

PREFACE.

WHAT may be called the text of this little volume was taken from the lips of Richard Hampton by Mr. Thomas Garland, formerly of Cambridge, Illogan, Cornwall. The manuscript which came into the hands of Thomas Garland, of Fairfield, in the same parish, was, after his decease, entrusted to the Editor by Mrs. Garland, who suggested that, if it were published in connection with living recollections of Richard's person, character, manners, and talk, it would be welcome to those who cherish the autobiographer's memory, while it might be interesting and instructive to all who love to trace the Divine Spirit's operation upon peculiar varieties of human character.

Richard's dictations are given as far as possible in his own style, and are rendered in accordance with his peculiar tone and pronunciation, as far as these could be expressed by the pen. His quotations from Holy Scripture are, in due reverence for the sacred text, given in the rendering of our English Bible; and the extracts from his favourite hymns are after the version commonly used. The renderings of his own talk will, it is hoped, be generally understood by the aid of a few bracketed explanations. The personal recollections of the Editor are interwoven with the text, or given in the closing chapters, associated with testimonies from others who knew Richard in his later life, and who witnessed the close of his mortal course.

This attempt to give something like a fair sketch of a singular character, and to preserve the memory of one, in the development of whose intellect, and in the regulation and fruitfulness of whose energies the Spirit of Christ so remarkably exemplified his power, will not fail of its purpose, if it help to refresh kind recollections of the departed, or call forth from a single heart some new devotional acknowledgment of Him, who, at times, as in the case of Richard Hampton, "hath chosen the foolish things of the world to confound the wise."

S. W. C.

REDRUTH, *March*, 1873.

FOOLISH DICK.

CHAPTER I.

DICK'S FAMILY LINE AND FIRST APPEARANCE IN THE WORLD.

BETWEEN forty and fifty years ago, anybody who was used to move about among the villages and hamlets of West Cornwall, and was in any way familiar with the religious doings of the mining and rural population, would every now and then meet with a remarkable personage, whose name, as a wandering preacher, was always enough to bring a crowd together wherever a meeting-place could be secured.

Once to see the man was never to forget him. A figure rather short, but thick and heavy, seeming the shorter from being so thick, and looking thicker and more heavy than it really was, because of the large and loose style of the garments which wrapped it. There was a long coat, by no means of tight fit; a waistcoat, like the long vests of a former generation, doubled over the broad corpulent front, and hanging above the lower garment, which was loosely buttoned at the massive knees, and covered with its ample folds the short and disproportioned limbs that helped the man to shuffle onward rather than to walk. When seen moving on the road, with his large weather-beaten hat low over his brow, he would attract attention as being singular in appearance and manner rather than very vigorous, active, or fruitful in intellect. But to look at him uncovered, and to hear his voice was to discover that his mental character and soul's history were even more peculiar than the shaping of his outer man. His head and face might be called massive. His heavy, well-nourished shaven chin, which would be taken as indicating a disposition to sluggishness or lethargy, was more than balanced by his broad and lofty brow, with its short-cut, uncared-for crown of hair. His eyes, glistening from beneath their overhanging shelter, were indescribable, and when in full and most expressive action, were curiously correspondent with his other features in revealing the strange combinations of his character. It was difficult to know which eye looked at you. One had a twist or squint, which seemed to have an endless variety of meaning, and to express at command a sly, or comical, or humorous, or inquisitive, or solemn thought; and often helped, in a resistless way, to give point to his retorts, force to his appeals, and life to the apothegms that would break forth in his private talk or public discourse.

Out of his own county he was sometimes spoken of as "the Cornish Fool"; nearer to home he was known to some as "Foolish Dick," to others as "the Foolish Preacher." But those who knew him best and loved him for his Master's sake, gave him a local title expressive of endearment or veneration, and called him "Uncle Richard." Many had cause to hold him dear, and by many more his character and memory would be venerated.

Nobody who had seen Richard Hampton, or had heard him speak or pray, would be without a wish to know something of his beginning and of the circumstances of his early life. He had sprung from one of those families of Cornish miners whose native force of character had been brought into consistent and happy action under the influence of Divine Truth, so as to mark them as religiously gifted households. In Dick's account of his family he says—

My faather's naame was John Hampton. He was a pooar man, an' wurked under groun' aall hes life. 'Twas some time 'fore he begun to sarve the Lord weth aall hes hart, I reck'n. While he was harty, an' had nothin' the matter wed'n, he keept back, an' wud'n gev up to God; but he liked to heear the praichers, and thoft (thought) much of 'em. I used to see un go away, when he cud, in a quiet plaace to pray. Tho', when hes cumraades (comrades) got hould ov un, aall the good was drawve out of hes mind. He went on like thes, to an agen, like the door on hes henges, haaltin' 'tween two openyuns (opinions). At laast he was brock down weth haard levvin' an' wurkin' in the wets an' damps; and, weth another world afore un, he gove up hes hart to the Sperrit's grace, I b'lieve he ded. It was in the 'eer 1796 that Cap'n Garland put on a class mittin' in our plaace. Faather went, an', as Maaster Garland was gevvin' out the hemn, faather stoppt un, and, says he, "Say ut ovver agen, ef you plaise; that's my feelin'." Thaise was the words:—

"Give me my sins to feel,
And then my load remove;
Wound, and pour in my wounds to heal,
The balm of pardoning love."

Soon arter that he took to hes bed. The night afore he died he caaled aall our family to un—muther, fower sons, and waun daughter—and tould 'em to be kind to waun anuther, to lev in paice, and every waun to be dootiful to muther. Then he prayed, and gove hes sawl to God; an', for the laast time, said to aall of us, "I wish 'ee well," and depaarted in paice.

Captain Garland, of whom Dick speaks, was the venerable father of the late well-known Thomas Garland, of Fairfield, and to him we are indebted for the pages of Richard's autobiography. He took the story from Dick's lips, and made the jottings which are now before us. Dick had a remarkable memory. Dates and particular events seemed to be printed in his mind like the pages of an almanack. One illustration may serve to show at once the minute accuracy of his recollection, and the wit with which he could cover an occasional failure. An old friend met with him one December afternoon, and wishing to test his memory, asked whether he could tell at what time the new moon came in for each past month of the year. Unknown to Dick, the friend had a circular-shaped almanack fitted into the crown of his hat, and holding it so as to command the figures for each month as he named it, he said—

"Now, Uncle Richard, can you tell me?"

"Iss, I reck'n."

"Well then, begin."

Six or seven months were correctly given, then there was an error.

"You are wrong, Richard."

"No, I reck'n."

"Well, who shall decide between us?"

"I b'lieve I knaw, I b'lieve I'm right."

"No, Richard, you can't be. See, here is the almanack; that must be right. And if that is right, you are wrong."

"Aw, my deear," was the quick response, "my knawledge es in my head, yours es awnly in your hat."

With such a memory for minute particulars, Dick would naturally weave dates and seeming trifles into his narrative; and he shows his distinctive readiness for this in the style of his first autobiographical record.

I was born on Thursday, April the 4th, in the 'eer 1782, on Nancekuke Down, in the parish of Luggan (Illogan) and county of Cornwall. When I cum into this world I was a braave, healthy cheeld, and promised to do well, havin' no waikness that cud be seen at aall. But I had not ben in thes vaale of teears, I had'n, more than seven weeks 'fore it plaised God to afflect me. I was took weth fits, which keept on 'pon me ever so long. Many times faather an' muther thoft that the vittal spaark was quinched, but as they watched by my craadle I shud cum to myself agen. So I keept alive tell the desmal fits left me. But they ded'n go without laivin' thear maarks. My sight was turned, my faace and lembs twested, and every paart of me, inside an' out, in such a shaape (confusion) that, as I grawed and went about, they that ded'n knaw me said, "That theere boay es haaf a fool, or more than that, he es." And 'twor all the wus for me, becaase I cud git nothin' but poor things to weear, awnly a few rags; an' in wenter it was busy all (all was needed) to keep me from shevverin'. They looked at me as fet for nothin', and thoft that I shud haave to drag along thro' life an idyat (idiot) like, tell God was plaised to taake me out of ut. My mind was like a thing shuck to rags, an' to this day I caan't recollect nothin' in my life 'fore I was ight (eight) 'eers owld.

My paarents then sent me to a raiding school, keept by a poor owld man caaled Stephen Martin. My schoolin' cost three a'pence a-week. I was keept theere for seven months, and so my edication was wuth no less than three shellin' and sexpence—theere's for 'ee! When my edication was fenished, as they do say, I was took hum, seven months' larning bein' aall that my poor paarents cud affoord for me.

But I shall have to bless God to aall eternaty for that edication. At that deear owld man's school I larnt to raid a book they caaled a Psalter; an', havin' larnt so fur, when I got hum I gove myself to raidin', and keept on keepin' on tell I cud raid a chaapter in the Testament or Bible.

Aw, my deear! what a blessin' thes heere larning a' ben to the poor idyat!

Yes, blessing indeed; it made the reputed fool wise—wise enough to gain happiness for himself, and wise enough to win souls. Dick's history and experience afford a beautiful illustration of the Divine words, "For whosoever hath to him shall be given, and he shall have more abundance." What a lesson for those who have the privilege of higher culture! The comparative fool improves seven months' instruction in a three-halfpenny school, till his knowledge of the Sacred Scriptures became large and deep enough to shame the ignorance of reputed masters in learning.

When Dick became known as a preacher, he was remarkable for his knowledge of the Sacred Scriptures, and for his shrewd, happy, and effective mode of expounding and applying the holy text which lived in his memory and heart. Even before he was so publicly engaged as a preacher and exhorter, he was often more than a match for the cleverest among those who sometimes ventured to play with what they supposed to be his pretensions to Bible learning. One illustration occurs. He was one day waiting in the office of an influential firm, having been sent on a business errand by his friend and employer.

"Richard," said one of the gentlemen, "they say you know a good deal about the Bible; go home and look, and you will find in the fourth chapter of Habakkuk a passage that will do for a text for you: the words are, 'Rise, Jupiter, and snuff the moon!'"

"No, maaster, I doan't b'lieve that they words are in the Bible," he replied, "and theere es no moare than three chapters in Habakkuk, nuther; but I d' knaw that in the ighteenth verse of the twenty-second chapter of Revelation you'll find thaise words, 'If any man shall add unto these things, God shall add unto him the plagues that are written in this book.'"

His knowledge of the Old Testament, too, was sufficiently full and certain to enable him sometimes to quote with great readiness, so as to express his humour, or indicate his own wishes, or his notion of what it became other people to do. He had been sent one day on an errand to the "count-house" of a mine. He arrived just as the dinner was served up for the officials. A roast shoulder of mutton was laid on the table. Dick was tired and hungry. The sight of the dinner sharpened his appetite. But having delivered his message, the captain said to him—

"Sit down, and you shall have some dinner by-and-bye."

He sat and watched the privileged staff at their meal, until, prompted by growing desire, he said, "Cap'n Tom, do 'ee knaw what Samuel towld the cook to do for Saul?"

"No, Dick; what was it?"

"Why, 'Samuel said unto the cook, bring the portion which I gave thee; and the cook took up the shoulder and that which was upon it, and set it before Saul.'"

The hint was good-naturedly taken, and a portion from the shoulder was set before the hungry messenger.

But let Dick himself be heard again respecting his boyhood:—

About thes time that Sperrit that gove light when God said "Let there be light" sent light into my mind. Thofts about God wud keep coming up in me, an' I ded'n knaw how to tell 'em out; I had no words for 'em. Howsomever, I had the thofts, and deep wauns too, I had. I've got up many times out of bed in the dead o' might, and while the rest of 'em wud be slaipin' I used to git out, and for th' coose of an hour and moare look at the moon and the staars, and think about He that maade 'em. And aw, my deear, I caan't help thenkin' that they thofts that I had out of a night worn't so much my awn as the Sperrit's, like.

I rec'lect waunce, when about nine 'eers owld, waun hevvening, theare was another boay weth me, and we wore lyin' down 'pon the common, glaazing (gazing) up at the sky, when he towld me that the whoal world and aall 'round un wud waun day catch fire and burn away. I got frightened, and run hum and towld faather, an' he towld me that "the earth and all the works therein" shud be burnt up. This went thro' me, and was the fust feelin' that drawve me to pray.

'Pon another occayon, when Maaster Wesley praiched at the pit, and aall the neighburs wore flockin' away to heear'n, that theare saame hevvening my sawl was so titched that I stayed up ever so laate consederin' the hevvens and the staars that God's fengers had maade.

In thes heere way, while I was hum, my life paassed along braave an' comfor'ble, and I had many putty times of ut. But my paarents was poor, and every sexpence was of vally (value), so, as soon as cud be, I was caaled to work to help 'em. I was 'bout eleven 'eers owld when I was hired out to tend the Rickers at the stampses (stamping mills), for three shellin' and sexpence a month. I was awnly glad to git anything for faather an' muther, the deears. But aw my time was spent in laabour an' sorrow, sure 'nough. Many times ded I go and cum from work weth baare feet, and my poor thin body with nothin' but rags 'pon me. Some people ded pity me, they that had feelin'. But aw the wecked boays ded nothin' but loff, and everything they cud do they ded to maake my sufferin's bitterer. They wud scat (strike) my lembs, an' teear my cloase. Sometimes they wud git 'round me in a ring, and tell me that ef I wud sweear they wud lev me aloane, and not taize me never no moare. Then they wud tie my hands behind my back, an' put a hank'shuff ovver my eyes, an' caal me haaf-saaved, and foach (push) agen me, an' then they wud say that ef I wud but sweear they wud lev me go. But I wud'n. I was all'ays keept from that sin. I never, in aall my life, swoar an oath, an' I remember that, ef any body caaled at my faather's, I used to ax, arter he was gone, whether he wore a sweearer. Sweearing all'ays ded simmee (seem to me) an awful sin, an' I'm afeer'd o' my life to this day to heear God's naame took in vain.

I wurked at the stampses, and had vaaryus gittings, tell I was ighteen, but I never cud do anything but wheeling, and things like that. I cud'n larn any aisy wurk, nor git to knaw how to do ut. From the stampses I went to wurk weth Maaster John Phillips, a faarmer in our parish, an' he gove me fust ninepence and then 'leven pence a day. Maaster an' missis wore very kind; they had larnt to govern by love. I had a shilter now from the boays at the stampses, and had a bit of time, to an' agen, for good thofts and prayer, an' I feelt that I was gitting aall the better. Ef the feelds an' copses, an' the downses, an' the furzy braakes, the caaves, the cleffs, an' sandy banks cud spaike, they cud tell many of my poor prayers. I had keept up my seeryus thofts aall thro' my troubles at the stampses, and was 'termined to sarve the Lord. So I joined in the class mittin', and keept on for two or three months, tell I thoft how that I was so deffernt to other people that my class maates cud'n like me, and cud'n look 'pon me as waun of 'em, like. Thes thoft brock me down, and I gove up the mittin'. But now I was under Maaster Phillips I got comfor'ble. 'Twas good to pray now, et was, an' my sawl clinged to God an' Hes people. I gove 'em my heart an' hand to live and to die weth 'em.

Dick's account of his own devotional pursuits at

this period of his life is deeply interesting, and may awaken many a touching reflection on the Fatherly goodness of Him who watched and waited in the hollows of the common, the holes of the rocks, and on the sands of the shore to hear the broken utterances of the poor, persecuted, crippled, and impotent lad. Recollections of him and his mode of life, at the time alluded to, are cherished even now around the scenes where he used so curiously to interweave prayer and pious thought with imperfect efforts at unskilled labour. There still floats many a story of his devout manner of improving little suggestive circumstances.

On passing the gate of a pious neighbour one day, as he went to the well for water, the neighbour nodded to him, and said—

"So you are going to the well for water, Dick?"

"Iss."

"Do you know that the woman of Samaria found Jesus at the well?"

"Ded she?" was the only response; but the thought was fixed. And as he went, that thought quickened into holy desires, and the seemingly silly water-carrier said within himself—

"Why shud'n I find Jesus at the well?"

Jesus met him there; and that well-side was numbered with Dick's other holy closets among the furze bushes, and beneath the sand-banks and silent rocks.

CHAPTER II.

DICK'S EARLY DAYS OF LABOUR, SORROW, AND JOY.

DICK'S early days were days of painful drudgery and persecution. Nor was he entirely without trials during his days of protected retirement in the service of Mr. John Phillips. His story continues:—

The awnly persecution I mit weth while wurking weth Maaster Phillips, was waun day when going to the smeth's shop to git my tool shaarpened; some wecked young men laid hould ov me, and tied me to a caart's tail, an swoar that they wud draaw me to Faa'mouth (Falmouth) an' put me boord a man-o'-war. They draaged me for haalf a mile, an' at laast the rope brawk an' I 'scaaped out of thear hands. Howsomever, aall the time they keept draawing me I had paice in my sawl, I had.

About thes time my laider was very eernest weth me to gev myself no rest tell I knawed that God loved me sure 'nough. I 'tended to hes advice, and gove myself to moare prayer than ever. At waun class-mittin' that was in May, 1804, everybody in the mittin' feelt uncommon power of the Sperrit. I was 'termined nevver, nevver to gev up tell I knawed for sartin that I had the love of God in my sawl. I was goin' the day arter and many moare, not awnly prayin', to and agen, but weth a soart of continned prayer. Waun afternoon I got out into a pit on the downs, and theere I wrastled mightily weth the Lord. My sawl was in an agony; I ded wrastle! For an hour and haalf I keept at ut; and at laast the kingdom of hevven was revailed to my belaivin' heart. Aall my feears waalked off clain: my sawl was aall fresh an' noo, I was happy sure 'nough. Jesus was so butaful to me, I was full ov love to He an' every waun. I was bowld to sing—

> "Lame as I am, I take the prey;
>   Hell, earth, and sin with ease o'ercome;
> I leap for joy, pursue my way,
>   And as a bounding hart fly home;
> Through all eternity to prove
> Thy Nature and Thy Name is Love."

Nevver ded a thusty man long for cleear spring waater moare than I ded now for the next class-mittin'. My sawl waanted to powr foath the rapshur I feelt; an' when the time ded cum, aw, my cup was full and runnin' ovver! Aw, how I cud spaik of Hes love! I tould 'em aall, I ded, without feear, what God had done for me— iss, for poor me, that they do caal "haaf-saaved Dick." 'Tes no haaf-saaved Dick now! The Lord gove me not a haaf but a whoal salvaashun—'tes salvaashun to the uttermoast, et 'tes!

The genuineness of Richard's spiritual piety was to have continuous testing amidst the trials to which his singular appearance, manners, and limited ability for the ordinary work of life necessarily exposed him. His account is—

I wurked weth Maaster Phillips about three 'eers, when I left he and went to sarve anuther maaster; but aw, here ded begin trials and sufferin's. My maaster keept a lot o' moyles (mules) to car' cawls (coals) and copper oore, an' my wurk was to go weth the caryur to fill the sacks and help un to git the moyles along. Heere I got the wecked boays an' girls round me agen; they knackt me about, thraw'd stoanes at me, shoved me into mud pools; an' waun day, as I was goin' along by a church, I was draagged into the tower an' locked up ever so long. Many, many miles have I lemped along arter the moyles ovver the stony roads weth not a shoo to my foot nor a bit of anything 'pon my back that wud keep out the cowld and wet.

Waun mornin' maaster towld me that the caryur was sick and cud'n go weth the moyles, but he wud git a man to put the saddles on, and then I shud drive 'em to the mine. I towld un I cud'n do ut, nor more cud I. He swoare out 'pon me and said I shud; so he towld 'em to git all the moyles reddy 'cept two, and they he towld me to drive to feeld. Now, thoft I, es my time. I drawve the moyles to feeld, and then I runned for my life—aw, I ded run, I ded; and at laast I got down to the sayside, and theere I clucked (crouched) down cloase tell I thoft that maaster had gove up sarching for me; 'pon that I waalked to my owld maaster's faarm plaace—Maaster John Phillips—an' he took me into sarvice agen. I shud nevver 'a runned away from my laast maaster ef he had'n swoare 'pon me becaase I wud'n do what I cud'n—I knawed I cud'n do ut, an' God knawed too, for aall thro' He gave me paice, and I cud love every fellaw-craitur; and I nevver stopped away from my class-mittin' nuther, not waunce.

I was in Maaster John Phillips's sarvice

tell he gove up the faarm, an' then I went to wurk weth Maaster Hugh Phillips. A kind maaster he was, but my fellaw-sarvants traited me very bad, and arter six weeks I left that plaace.

Richard's very limited capacity for ordinary labour was his affliction; but, in many cases, it was suspected to be his fault. The thoughtless and indiscriminating were sometimes disposed to say of him, "He es haaf a fool, ef not wus; and laazy 'nough for a gen'leman." It was surmised by some that his inability for any skilled work was affected as a cover for sloth; but few took pains to trace his failures to the curious effect of physical derangement by early fits upon those mental faculties, the healthy and regular action of which is necessary to skilled labour. The twist in Dick's sight might be the visible indication of that inward twist which left him a shrewd thinker on some sides of a question, while it crippled him for dealing with others. Some true tales of him may serve to illustrate the grotesque association in his system of order and disorder.

One of his masters conceived that he might be capable of orderly thought in manual labour, so far, at least, as to distribute manure properly over the surface of a field. He was put to work in the morning and fairly instructed how to wheel out the manure from the heap in the corner of the field, and drop the several barrowfuls in smaller heaps at certain distances, so that when the whole was thus laid out, the manure might be scattered from the smaller heaps over the entire space. Dick was left to his work. But in the evening, the manure was found still in a large heap in the corner, as it had been in the morning.

"Why, Dick," said the master, "you have done nothing all the day."

"Iss I have, maaster," was the prompt reply, with a look of mingled humour and self-content; "iss I have; I ded aall you towld me, and feneshed by denner time; but I thoft it wud'n do to taake a whoal day's waages for a haaf-day's wurk, so, arter denner, I wheeled ut aall back agen!"

He had been put to weeding work in the garden, too, and particularly shown how to distinguish the young leeks, or onions, or raddishes, from the weeds. The result was the dismay of the employer, when Dick, with a kind of triumphant light in his squinting eye, pointed to the entirely tenantless beds, emptied alike of weeds and crops, and said, "Theere now, I've done un butaful, and weeded un clain!" Dick proved, however, now and then, that he was not without thought, tact, and skill, or faithfulness either, in certain lines of business action. He tells his own tale:—

Arter I gove up in the laast faarm plaace,

my laider, bein' aagent in East and North Towan Mines, he took me into hes employ, in goin' arran's, carrin' letters and goods, and the like a that; and theere I was saafe from parsecushun, 'cept now and then on the rooads. My laider was my shilter, and nobody cud mislest (molest) me nuther.

In the five 'eers that I sarved my laider I had lots of marcies: many friends I found both to body and sawl. I was not wethout caals to cumbat nuther. Some thoft that I was a braave fool, an' used to loff and try to puzzl' me; but I b'lieve the Lord helped me all'ays, and gove me to aanswer " fools according to their folly."

Waunce I was goin' to Tuckingmill, and a gen'leman—I s'pose he was—cum up an' says to me, loffing like, " An' wheere dedst thou cum from?"

" I cum from the dust, says I, an' am goin' to dust agen, the same as thee art!"

Simmee hes faace aaltered, an' he left me to keep my awn rooad.

Those who sometimes ventured to assail Dick while on the road doing his errands, did not always come off from the encounter so easily as the poor gentleman whose face altered under the fool's rebuke.

His ingenuity and wit sometimes took other turns as circumstances called them out to secure supplies or in self-defence. He was not always in so grave a mood. On one occasion he was in attendance at the mine, when a large party of adventurers were dining in the "count-house." As the cloth was removed, the captain asked the servant how Dick was getting on.

"I doan't knaw," said she, "but he do waant somethin' to drink, I reck'n."

"Why do you think so?"

"Becaase he a' ben maakin' poatry."

"Poetry! what has he said?"

"Why, a said—

> 'Ef aall the land was paaper,
> An' aall the say (sea) was ink,
> An' aall the trees wore bread an' cheese,
> What shud us do for drink?'"

Dick's need was forthwith supplied; and then the company wished him to be called in. He was brought to sit between two London adventurers; and after several queer questions and more queer replies, his right hand man said, "Dick, they say that you are more R than F."

"What do 'ee main, plaise?" asked Richard.

"Mean?" said the one on his left, "we want to know whether you are a rogue or a fool?"

"Why," said Dick, casting a squint first on one side and then on the other, "'tween the two, I reck'n!"

There were times, also, when Richard showed himself capable, not merely of keen retort in a playful way, but of ready smartness in calculations, and unlooked for shrewdness and tact in business affairs. One or two illustrations are given from his own lips.

Waun day I was in a gen'leman's office and the claarks axed me what waages I got; says I, waun thousen' seven hunderd an' twenty-three fard'ns a month. The gen'leman heeard this — he was a 'venterer (adventurer) in our mine—an' he said that my Cap'n oft (ought) to gev me two thousen' fard'ns a month. I towld my laider of ut when I got back, and he rawse my waages to forty shellin' a month; that' was waun thousen' nine hunderd and twenty fard'ns, nigh 'pon what they spok for at the office.

I deearly loved my Cap'n, and when

things prospered weth he, I feelt as ef 'twore the saame weth me; an' when things looked wisht, (melancholy) like, weth Cap'n, et was desmal times weth me. Waun day he sent me on a arrand to anuther mine. When I cum into the count-house the aagent was setting to brekfast, an' he begun to ax me 'bout a mine that I knawed was poor at that time, and gove but malancolly prospic. I knawed what he wanted to find out, so says I to he—

"Do 'ee knaw what the apostle says?"

"No," says he; "what es ut?"

"Why," says I, "'Whatsoever is set before you, eat, asking no questions, for conscience sake.'"

That was 'nough for he; he went on faaster than ever clunking (swallowing) hes brekfast, and ded'n stop to ax me any moore quesshuns 'pon that head.

'Twore while I was at the mine that my deear faather depaarted thes life, an' when he died the putty little premises we had was gone, faaling into the lord's hands when the laast life in the laise dropped. Theere was a tidy little house an' fowr smaal plots of land. My brothers cud'n pay for anuther laise, but, like the sons of Jacob, they stud lookin' waun 'pon anuther, not knawing what to do; not knawing how to laive the plaace which deear owld faather had got for us weth the sweat of his brow; and not knawing, nuther, wheere to find shilter for ourselves an' deear owld muther, who was left. But heere, too, the Lord was "a present help in trouble." My deear friend went to the steward for us, an' he promised that we shud have the owld plaace still on raisonable terms. The way 'twore done was thes: my brothers keept me in mait an' cloase, and I gove up my thousen' nine hunderd an' twenty fard'ns a month into the hands of the steward tell we had paid aall that he axed.

So I went on my way, doin' whatsomever my Cap'n towld me at the mine by day, and goin' to mittin's ov a hevvening, when my day's work was ovver. And 'twore by keepin' to the public mains of graace, and reg'lar 'tendance at my class, that the life of God was keept in my sawl.

At the time I was convarted noane of my brothers was reledjus, an' I cud'n go into my closet in my awn hum and shut the door. But I found a plaace. I went out 'pon the downs, and digged out a caave in the side of a smaal hill like, and theere I cud git in out of the world weth my Bible and Hemn book, and wait 'pon God in paice and quiet. Iss, theere I used to go, and in dead of wenter I wud taake a showl (shovel) and showl away the snaw from the mouth of my little caave, to git into my deear retrait. Theere I have had sweet uneyon an' communeyon weth my Hevvenly Faather, and theere I have renude my strength for the way, and got pow'r an' graace to do my wurk an' to suffer my Saaviour's will.

'Mong aall the members of hes class, my laider thoft that I was the laast waun to look to for to be useful in any public way. But waun day, while we wore in company, I towld un theere was somethin' in my mind that towld me that I shud be a soart of witness for Christ. He knawed I was senceare, but looked 'maazed like at what I said. He knawed how I gove myself to prayer, and thoft to ax me to pray in the class-mittin'. He ded so waun Sunday mornin', an' the Lord gove me such power that from that time my deear laider feelt that the Lord had wurk for me to do. He maade some trials of me, and then gove me a plan to 'tend prayer-mittin's; an' I went reg'lar, an' found that the blessed Sperrit was weth me.

Here, then, was the simple primitive training school in which Dick first learnt to exercise that gift of prayer for which he became so remarkable. He must have had that native combination of meditative power, warm feeling, and facile expression which, as natural endowments, are necessary to success in public prayer or exhortation. But these scarcely discovered themselves in Richard, or, at least, were never brought out in their full proportions and effective play, till his heart came entirely under the hallowing influence of religion. Not until the love of God became his ruling principle and chief joy were his native faculties found equal to the utterance of public prayer. The Spirit of God, as he said, was with him; and his gift of prayer was among the gifts of the Holy Ghost. Like those who " spoke with other tongues " under pentecostal blessing, Dick found fresh powers of utterance when love prompted him to pray with his neighbours.

His brothers, too, when brought under the same renewing and sanctifying power, became remarkable for their gift of prayer. Indeed the gift might almost seem to be distinctive of the family. How many times have the thrilling voices of those praying men been welcomed in " the great congregation " at Redruth! In other respects comparatively uncultured, their thoughtful, reverent, and appropriate appeals to God have so richly expressed the various desires of the people, as to result in blessings even upon following generations. Those voices of prayer have long since passed into immortal praise; but they have left sacred tones still lingering in the souls of those who revere their memory. In the gifts of such men, and in the divine responses to their devotion, there are at once bright illustrations and rich fulfilments of a noble intercessory hymn.

> "Come in Thy pleading Spirit down,
>   To us who for Thy coming stay;
> Of all Thy gifts we ask but one,
>   We ask the constant power to pray·
> Indulge us, Lord, in this request,
> Thou canst not then deny the rest."

CHAPTER III.

DICK'S INTRODUCTION TO PUBLIC LIFE.

IT was soon found that Richard's gift of prayer was not his only talent. He who taught him to speak to God in behalf of men, endowed him with power to speak to men the truth of God. In his case, as well as others, it was seen to be true, that, the nearer to God the nearer to man. His call and first efforts as a preacher are recorded by himself:—

I was thirty 'eers of aage, when aall at waunce, in a way that I ded'n ever look for, I was fo'ced out to caal sinners to repentance; an' I was soon foath in the highways and hedges, in the feelds and straits, baarns an' market-plaaces, by the way-side, in chaapels, an' anywheere that I cud git people to heear the noos of salvaashun.

Now, the way I was fust drawve out es like thes heere. My Cap'n sent me weth a letter to Redruth poast-offis; the letter had a bill in un wuth a hunderd poun's. Cap'n towld me to be sure I gove un in aall saafe, an' then to car' a noate to Maaster Joseph Andrew. I ded so, but while I was stannin' at hes door tell I had hes aanswer, a young wumman, as she was washin' the wenders (windows) glazed at me, an' says she, "That theere young man can look *ninety-nine* ways at waunce." Says I to she, "What man, having an hundred sheep, if he lose one of them, doth not leave the *ninety and nine* in the wilderness and go after that which is lost, until he find it? and when he hath found it, he layeth it on his shoulders rejoicing. And when he cometh home, he calleth together his friends and neighbours, saying unto them, rejoice with me, for I have found my sheep which was lost. I say unto you that likewise joy shall be in heaven over one sinner that repenteth, more than over *ninety and nine* just persons that need no repentance."

Some boays stannin' near, got in 'round me, an' at laast a mob gethered, and they foached (pushed) me down the strait. In the por (bustle) I lost my hat; tell gittin' cloase to a mait-stannin' (shambles), to saave myself from bein' stanked (trampled) under fut, I got up and set down 'pon the stannin'; an' then, aw, I feelt my sawl all a-fire weth love for everybody theere, and sprengin' to my feet, I begun to ex'ort, and then took to pray. Soon as I spok they wore aall quiet; norra waun had a word to say, an' they looked seeryus, an' at laast teears begun to run: aw, what a plaace et was—'twas "the house of God" sure 'nough. My sawl was so happy! everybody wud cum foath simmin to shaw how kind they cud be. They got my hat for me agen, and some of 'em wud gev me money ef I wud taake ut; but no, 'twas'n silver or gowld that I looked for. I was happy, and full of love, and in that staate I went back hum.

The spot on which Dick stood to give his first exhortation might well be deemed a consecrated one. There, for many years, Wesley used to take his stand and lift up his voice to "thousands upon thousands"; sometimes finding "scarce any (but gentlemen) who were not convinced of the truth;" sometimes "extremely weary, and the friends so glad to see him that none ever thought of asking him to eat or drink." Again, when "God seemed to be moving in all the hearts of the multitude;" again, when the parish parson "interrupted him by reading the riot act;" and, at last, when, as the fruit of his labour, "the roughest had become one of the quietest towns in England." On that same spot afterwards appeared Joseph Benson, the commentator, preaching with a power unusual even with him; and as one of his hearers, now in Paradise, used to say, "while he weighed character after character in the balances, and cried with a piercing voice as one after another was found deficient, 'wanting! wanting! wanting!' the people fell as if mowed down rank after rank, until the picturesque old street became like a scene in Pentecost." There, again, at a later period, says the same witness, "market-people were seen to drop their baskets in the place of business, that they might unite in cries for Divine mercy, or in praise and thanksgiving for present salvation." And now, from among the children of those who owed their spiritual life, under God, to scholars, gentlemen, and Christians, like Wesley and Benson, there rises up from amidst the mischievous rabble the partly-imbecile son of a common miner witnessing on the same spot to the same truth as Wesley and Benson preached; filled with the same Spirit, and speaking with like saving power. Verily, Redruth Street might be vocal with striking lessons on the claims of Him to whom alone it belongs from generation to generation to "thrust out labourers into His harvest." He sees not as man sees. And the history of the true succession of divinely-appointed Christian agencies affords most instructive evidence that the Head of the Church often makes but little account of mere human principles of organisation for holy work. In His choice of workmen, and in their training and adaptation, He seems to be ever saying, "I will destroy the wisdom of the wise, and will bring to nothing the understanding of the prudent. Where is the wise? Where is the scribe? Where is the disputer of this world? Hath not God made foolish the wisdom of this world? The foolishness of God is wiser than men, and the weakness of God is stronger than men. So that no flesh should glory in His presence; but according as it is written, he that glorieth, let him glory in the Lord."*

* 1 Cor. xix. 19—31.

Dick's successful beginning from the market-stall seemed to betoken his future calling. It was proved that he had gifts; he enjoyed, without doubt, the grace of love, and the penitent tears of his first congregation were earnests of ripe and lasting fruit.

He goes on with his story:—

When I was fo'ced out like thes heere at fust, I knawed that God had awpened a door for me to praich Hes Word, an' I went foath. Theere was a prayer-mittin' ovver to Luggan Highway soon arter I had spok in Redruth, and as no praying cumraades (comrades) was theere, I gove a word of ex'ortashun agen, an' the people got good to their sawls. But aw, twornt long 'fore some of our people rawse up agen me. The wust of 'em wore reledjus perfessurs, they wore. Aall soarts of taalk there was about my settin' up for a praicher. Some said that I shud maake a putty shaape (a pretty mess) ov ut, an' bring shaame 'pon reledjun. Others caaled me a fool. Many wore of openyon that I went about taalking 'cause I wud'n wurk. But, weth aall thes heere deffernce 'round me, theere wore some kind friends who spok in a loving way, and towld me to live neear to God, and He wud awn my laabour, and gev me sawls for my hire. Iss, weth aall that wore agen me, my hands wore maade strong by the mighty God of Jacob, an' I went on as far as I cud, taaking my friend's advice not to taake a tex, but to keep on ex'ortin' like, an' wrastlin' in prayer. 'Fore long I was axed to spaik at Tuckingmill, and theere was a laarge getherin', and they gove great attenshun. From theere I went to Carnkie, an' then to aall the smaal plaaces 'round Camborne. The Lord gove me strength to go wheere He awpened a plaace for me, and when the people was maade ready He drawve me foath. Theere was a caal to Marazion, an' theere Maaster Millet shawed great love, and got laive for me to spaik in the chaapel, an' the house was crowded.

Hayle-Copperhouse was my next plaace, an' lots got together to heear what I cud say in the naame of the Lord. They broft me to Godolphin mine, and theere, stannin' up in a buckin' house, the Lord gove me power to ex'ort hunderds of people. Just as I had stopped spaikin', a poor drunkard cum foath weth a glass of brandy in hes hand, and said a wud maake the praicher drink un. "No," says I, "you wean't, an' let me tell 'ee what the wise man says, 'The drunkard shall come to poverty, and drowsiness shall clothe a man with rags.'"* God's Word was 'nough for he, so he went on hes way.

My next round was Bodmin Circuit. Aw! that was a round, sure 'nough! I trampt ut thro' Luxillean, an' Roche, an' St. Dennis, an' St. Columb. In every plaace the deear people took me in, and shawed how they loved the Lord, by thear paashunce (patience) weth Hes poor sar-

---

* Proverbs xxiii. 21.

vent, an' the way they wud cum together an' howld me up weth thear prayers an' thear aigerness arter the Word of Life.

When I turned hum from thes eastern journey, I laaboured for a coose of time weth my deear owld laider. 'Tes pleasant to see noo faaces an' to find noo friends in straange plaaces; but owld friends cum very neear arter aall, an' my sawl was sperrited up, like, to heear my fust maaster in Christ pray agen, and taalk and taalk 'tell we shud bust foath in singin'—

> " All praise to our redeeming Lord,
>   Who joins us by His grace,
> And bids us each to each restored,
>   Together seek His face.
>
> " And if our fellowship below
>   In Jesus be so sweet,
> What height of rapture shall we know,
>   When round His throne we meet."

It is interesting to trace Dick to the scenes of his devout preparation for his public preaching-work abroad during the periods of his stay at home. Ever since his conversion in the pit on Nancekuke Downs, the pits on those downs seem to have been hallowed to him as his chosen retreats for spiritual exercise.

"We knew," says a witness, "that he spent a good deal of time somewhere on the common; and now and then a voice of prayer might be heard coming over the hill. But once when wandering over the downs, his earnest tones rose upon my ear from one of the pits. There he was pouring out warm utterances of truth. "Why, Richard," said I, stepping quickly forward, "what are you doing?"

"Preaching to myself," was his reply.

"Well, but you have no singers for your service."

"Iss, I have; doan't 'ee heear 'em?" said he, pointing upwards; "they 're up theere!"

They were the larks, high up, in full song.

Dear old Richard! he had an ear for the music of nature. His heart was in tune with the melodies of God's happy creatures. To his soul nature and grace sang in harmony.

His narrative continues :—

In the fust month of 1812 I was caaled to visit Porthleven, an' et was pleasant to laabour among the friends theere; an' from Porthleven I went foath an' spok to the people of Gunwallo, an' Mawgan, an' Cury, an' St. Kevern, an' Coverack, an' Constantine, an' Gweek, an' aall 'round they paarts.

Many sawls wore convenced, an' joined the people, an' are stiddy members to thes day, bless the Lord! My deear friends of Porthleven gove me a sute o' cloas—not afore 'twas needful nuther. My Heav'nly Faather all'ays sees to ut that I git what's needful in good time. "The Lord is my shepherd, I shall not want." I mit a man as I was goin' my roun's in my noo cloas, an' he axed me wheere I got my noo cloas; says I, "Wheere the raav'ns got thear feathers."

They wore kind to me at Porthleven; 'twas'n 'nough to cover my back, but they wud put money in my pocket too, the deears! I thoft to myself, "What shall I do weth thes heere?" so at leeast I boft a sheep weth ut; an' then, as ef the Lord wud maake me a rich man, He put up a friend to gev me anuther sheep; so I caaled waun of 'em *Purchase* and t'other *Freegift*, an' broft 'em hum to feed 'pon our downs.

When deear Maaster Stephens, of Breage,

left theere an' went to Sancreed, in the west, he sent for me to hes house, and gove out for a mittin' in hes baarn. Lots of the neighbours gethered, an' behaaved very daisent. From theere I was axed over to Mousehole. Aw, I ded tremble, I ded, an' feelt much afeared when I waalked up into the pulpet in that chaapel, an' theere was such a crowd of people too; and what was wus, as I thoft, theere wore aall the praichers—Maaster Haime, an' Maaster Scurrah, an' Maaster Sleep, an' Maaster Sibley. They wore cum for to heear me, how I cud git on. They wore kind, they wore, the deear men; and arter I had spok, they cum to me an' towld me that I had liberty to ex'ort in any plaace in the circuit wheeresomever I was axed to cum. Then I went foath and praiched in every chaapel about theere, an' " the power of the Lord was present to heal."* The friends wore wonderful kind; they had me from house

* St. Luke v. 17,

to house, an' gove me everything that cud be needed. For the loving kindness they shawed aall thro' thes journey, I pray God to remember 'em. Maaster Carne, an' Maaster Berriman, an' Maaster Kernick, an' Maaster Stephens, an' Maaster Jennings, the Lord look 'pon 'em aall for good, all'ays.

Dick did not always meet with such kind consideration, good sense, and judgment as were shown by his "deear men," Mr. Haime and his colleagues. At that time, as well as others, there were some who felt the full importance of their official standing, and who, on principle, sought to follow St. Paul's example, and "magnify their office." For such, Dick's shrewdness and native humour generally made him more than a match. One of these one day gave Dick to understand that he ought to know his place, and never to venture before chapel congregations without due recognition and sanction. The response was ready.

"I hope no 'ffence, I 'm sure. I ded'n knaw. I wud do all things ef I cud, 'decently and in order.'* You're a great man, you are, maaster, I knaw, an' a wise man, I 'spose. Now, maaster, don't 'ee fall

---

* 1 Cor. xiv. 40.

out weth a fool, for 'it pleased God by the foolishness of preaching to save them that believe.'* You are a larned man, too, I reck'n," he added, with one of those curious glances of his twisted eye which seemed to screw their way into one. "Can 'ee taalk Greek, maaster, can 'ee? Will 'ee plaise to say ovver a bit of ut to me?" Dick's squint and the comical turn of his lip made the question unmistakable. The official felt, perhaps, that he was unexpectedly brought to a standard of learning which he would rather not be measured by; and so, wisely taking Dick's advice, he let the "fool" have his way.

In his record of early pilgrimages as an exhorter, Richard, like patriarchial saints, carefully marked the places which to him were scenes of blessing, and gives the names of those who showed kindness to him on his way; though he gives few particulars as to the character or amount of his spiritual success. This seems to be rather from modesty than from lack of material or evidence. Those who have gone over the ground which he traversed on his errands of mercy have often found themselves amidst the permanent and living results of his simple and earnest toil. The fruit of his labour has been accumulative in many parts of the south and west of the county; and there still floats many a tale about the immediate saving effects of his power-

---

* 1 Cor. i. 21.

ful prayers, earnest public appeals, and private religious talk at the fire-side. His name is held sacred, and his memory is balmy in many a village, hamlet, and homestead; and very many happy spirits have passed up to meet him, as their spiritual father, in the presence of Him whose "strength was made perfect in his weakness."

Here and there, joyful stories of his hallowed successes have been found grotesquely associated with comic scenes in his itinerant life. The late Walter Lawry, the honoured pioneer missionary in the South Seas, himself keenly alive to the least touch of humour, and the slightest approach to the ridiculous, used to tell how he met with Dick, near the Lizard, rejoicing among the simple, happy souls who revered and loved him as an honoured instrument of blessing from God. By this time, notwithstanding his long exercise of legs and lungs, Dick had become more than comfortably corpulent. His energy, however, was unabated, and his zeal was still fresh and warm.

"Uncle Richard," said Lawry, "you must preach for me this evening."

"No, my deear maaster," was the reply, "I'm cum to hear you praich."

"You must preach, Richard; I shall take no denial."

Dick yielded at last, and he mounted the pulpit stairs. The door of that pulpit was uncommonly narrow, and in trying to enter, poor Dick stuck fast in the passage. He struggled, but, for a time, in vain. He could get neither in nor out. He was fairly trapped. He tugged and twisted, until, in spite of sympathy with his evident torture, his grotesque postures, and the indescribable contortions of his face, over which the sweat now trickled, irresistibly touched the congregation's sense of the ridiculous. Gravity was fairly overcome, and Dick's confusion was the more painfully deepened by the manifestations of public amusement. The difficulty was at last overcome; as soon as the preacher was within the pulpit, the tide of feeling changed. Dick seemed to gather fresh power of speech and resistless grace in prayer. He forgot his troubles, and the people were speedily lost to everything but joy in the truth and comfort in devotion. Richard was wisely patient, at the close of the service, till a few friends assisted him out of his confinement; and then throwing a queer look back on the scene of his struggle, he said, " Aw, shean't catch me in that soart of a trap, they shean't, never no more. Aall awpen doors ar'nt saafe wauns !"

CHAPTER IV.

DICK'S FIRST MOVEMENT OVER THE BORDER.

UNCLE RICHARD'S name soon became known beyond the limit of his native county. Rumours about his remarkable person and character, his power in prayer, and the saving results of his simple preaching had passed over the border into Devon, and some of the methodist folk in what was then called Plymouth Dock (now Devonport) determined, if possible, to secure an opportunity of seeing and hearing him for themselves.

Dick continues his tale:—

In the laater paart of the 'eer 1813, the friends at Plymouth Dock wore desirous that I shud vesit 'em, and sent letters to my laider, axing ov un to enform me ov ut, an' to send me up as soon as he cud. 'Bout ten days 'fore Chres'mas I got reddy for my journey. The thofts of goin' away so fur from hum wore raather hevvy 'pon my mind. At the class-mittin', 'fore I staarted, my sawl was draawed out in a wonderful manner for the convarshun of my deear owld muther an' my brothers. Arter I had gove 'em up to God, an' " to the word of His grace," I left hum in company weth waun who took me on as fur as Liskeard, an' theere gove me ovver into the chaarge of Maaster Pengelly, the wagginer, an' he broft me up to Tarpoint.

Poor Dick! he felt, as well as his friends, that on such a journey he should be in friendly charge and keeping. He was sufficiently apostolic in spirit and aim to find Christian friends, so far like primitive believers as to be ready " to bring him on his way" to his destined place of labour. Like many other simple-minded examples of zeal for Christ, Dick allowed no opportunity to pass on his way without efforts to promote the great object of his life. One of his fellow-travellers, in Mr. Pengelly's waggon, outlived him to tell the story of what occurred during the journey from Liskeard to Torpoint. The waggon was well filled. Dick was soon an object of deep interest and intense curiosity.

He sat on a rude seat across the carriage under the arched covering of thick woollen which at that time distinguished the style of conveyance for all who could not afford the luxury of a place inside or outside the stage-coach. For a time Dick seemed to be heedless of all around. Doubtless, the great venture on a journey like this was enough to absorb him, in connection, too, with the prospect of new scenes, strange faces, and work among somewhat polite congregations. He sat in his usual way, rocking to and fro on his seat, strangely twisting his features, and throwing oddly inquisitive glances from his oblique eye. As he waved, he hummed the tune of a favourite hymn; and now and then, in under-tones, would utter a verse or few words of his song—

> "How happy is the pilgrim's lot!
> How free from every anxious thought,
> From worldly hope and fear!
> Confined to neither court nor cell,
> His soul disdains on earth to dwell,
> He only sojourns here."

At length, during a short pause, a passenger, who could no longer restrain his inquisitiveness, turned to him and, half in jest, said, "Are you a tinker, sir?"

"No, hum-m-m.

> 'Nothing on earth I call my own;
> A stranger, to the world unknown,
> I all their goods despise;'"

Before he could sing out the verse, another traveller inquired, "Are you a shoemaker, sir?"

"No!

    'I trample on their whole delight,
      And seek a country out of sight,
        A country in the skies.'"

A third inquirer now determined, if possible, to be satisfied as to the character and calling of their strange companion, and with somewhat more of a respectful tone, said—

"Pray, sir, what may be your occupation?"

"Holiness es my caaling, ma'am!"

And then, raising his voice above the creaking and rumbling of the labouring waggon, he sang—

    "The things eternal I pursue;
     A happiness beyond the view
       Of those that basely pant
    For things by nature felt and seen;
    Their honours, wealth, and pleasures mean,
       I neither have nor want."

And before his astonished fellow-travellers could recover themselves so far as to pursue their inquiries, he looked around upon them, and with a sort of thundering voice, cried—

"My caaling es to caal sinners to repentance! 'Repent ye, therefore, and be converted, that your sins may be blotted out, when the times of refreshing shall come from the presence of the Lord!'"

The word rang through their very souls. There was deep silence, broken only by the tramp of the horses and the rattle of the wheels, until Dick's voice rose again with a repetition of the authoritative cry, "Repent!" The awe that crept over all held them in continued silence. Dick's "calling" was manifest in their consciences, and, though dumb, they seemed to agree in allowing the pilgrim preacher to fill up the remaining time of the journey with alternations of hymning, prayers, and exhortations. The songs, and prayers, and repetitions of inspired truths were not fruitless. The result was hallowed to one traveller at least. Dick had happily fulfilled his own calling.

The waggon arrived at Torpoint with its set of pondering passengers, and Richard's story goes on:—

When we wore cum to Tarpoint, I went down to the quay, an' the waatermen got 'round me, singing out—

"Want a booat, sir? want a booat, sir?"

"Iss," I towld 'em, "I do want a booat weth a tember bottom." They glazed at me, an' waun ov 'em took me into hes booat. As we wore crossing ovver the Hamoaze, I axed the waaterman, says I, "S'pose you do knaw aall about booats, doan't 'ee?"

"Iss," says he, "s'pose I do."

"Then," says I, "can 'ee tell how they maade the fust booat swem?"

"I'm sure I caan't tell," says he.

"Then," I said to un, "now s'pose you caan't tell 'fore we git ovver, I do think that you shud'n chaarge me anything for my paassage."

"We'll see 'bout that," says he.

At laast we got to North Corner, and then says I, "Can 'ee tell yet?"

"No, he cud'n," he said, "but 'fore you go," says he, "you must tell me how et was."

"Why, my deear man," says I, "doan't 'ee knaw how they maade the fust booat swem? Why, 'pon hes bottom, to be sure."

Aw, how he ded look! He got me out of hes booat as fast as he cud, and staared at me as ef he thoft I was maazed. 'Twas 'bout nine o'clock in the hevvening when I got 'pon the land, an' I begun to ax for

Maaster Richard Garland, and sure 'nough theere was a wumman theere, aall reddy to laid me to hes house. He was thenkful to God for bringin' me saafe on my journey, and so was I.

Next day Maaster Henshaw, the superintendant praicher cum to see me; an' when he was cum in, theere he keept stannin' glazing at me up and down, an' round, as ef he was misshurin' (measuring) ov me; and theere was I, looking at he too. At laast he axed me ef I cud say ovver any vesses (verses) of a hemn. I towld un I cud. "Well," says he, "let me heear 'ee." So I went ovver some. Then he axed me to repait some passiges of Scripshur, an' I ded so. He went on ever so long axing me vareyus things, an' then he went away. I doan't think, from hes looks, that he thoft much of the poor Cornish praicher. Well, I cud'n maake myself deffer'nt to what I was, an' I cud'n help ut ef he found me deffer'nt to what he had thoft to find.

'Fore he knawed much about me, he had gove out that the Cornish Fool was coming in a few days, and wud praich; and ef he found that I was a fool, sure 'nough what cud I help ut?

It might be wished that this first interview between Mr. Henshaw and Dick could have been photographed at the moment of its most comical interest. The somewhat precise and judicious superintendent minister, with something like prim notions of what is proper, and rather anxious as to his own reputation for official prudence, confronting the "Fool," with the awkward recollection of having publicly announced his speedy appearance before he had conceived what that appearance might possibly be. He was now face to face with the strange unanticipated reality, a presence which seemed to show that by publishing for the "Fool" before he had seen him, he might himself be chargeable with folly. The "Fool" was other than his fancy had pictured him. What now could be done? There was something true about the queer-fashioned preacher, yet something weird. What course should he take? He could not decide; and, perhaps, he thought it best to slip off for the present undecided, rather glad to get away from under the cross-fire of Dick's unparalleled eyes, whose glances, though never seemingly aimed certainly at him, yet never failed to make him feel their somewhat uncomfortably intrusive power.

Dick was permitted, at all events, to make his appearance in public. He continues his chronicle:—

Next hevvening I ex'orted at Stoke, in a smaal room, 'bout haalf a mile from Dock. Maaster Henshaw an' the other praicher heeard me. I had a missure of leberty. Maaster Henshaw went hum weth me, an' was simmin' more plaised like; he towld the congregaashun, 'fore they brok up, that I shud praich next morning in Morice Street Chaapel, at six o'clock—that was Chres'mas-day morning. Theere was a laarge getherin' sure 'nough. I spok from thaise words,— "For unto you is born this day, in the city of David, a Saviour, which is Christ the Lord."* The Lord gove me great en-laargement; He was weth us in a wonderful manner. "The power of the Lord was present," to wownd an' "to heal."† Maaster Henshaw hisself milted like waax afore the

---

* St. Luke ii. 11. † St. Luke v. 17.

fire—he cud'n howld out agenst ut; an' he took to me like a friend an' brother, an' thrawed hes arm 'round me, and laid me hum to hes house, an', simmin', cud'n do 'nough for the poor Cornish praicher. He was so full of love an' caare for me now. Aw, when the Sperrit do come, like He ded that Chres'mas mornin', He

"Scatters abroad,
Throughout every place,
By the least of His servants, the savour of grace."

Mr. Henshaw's scruples were all overcome by the power and unction which attended Dick's ministry; and it is as instructive to see the cautious man kindling into warmth, as Richard's hallowed powers unfold themselves in the manifested presence of the new-born Saviour, as it was amusing to watch his wonderment and perplexity at the first sight of the reputed fool. He who had been well-nigh classed and dealt with as belonging to those who "are esteemed as earthen pitchers, the work of the hands of the potter, was proved to be one of the precious sons of Zion, comparable to fine gold."* It is only as the soul is purified by the Spirit of grace, and is conformed to the Author of spiritual

---

* Lam. iv. 2.

life, beauty, and power, that it has capacity to discern spiritual life and beauty in its fellow-creatures. Only as far as it is in itself an object of Divine affection is it prepared to see and acknowledge true lovableness in human character. Only "the pure in heart see God." And the degree of a man's own pure Christian simplicity must be the measure of his insight into what is God-like in those who appear under the disadvantages of mortal weakness and physical disorder. The greater the outward disadvantages of the pure Christian, the more pure and vigorous must be the grace by which his inward beauty and virtue are seen, loved, and acknowledged.

Such was poor Dick's outer man, that there might be some excuse for one who did not at first sight see into the rudely-covered treasures of his soul. What was truly lovable in him was certainly not at once found on the surface. Nor would it be suspected, at a glance, that under such appearances manners, and address there lay such hallowed gifts for public usefulness.

Mr. Henshaw, like many others, needed more than one sight, more than one hearing, in order to discover how far the converting and sanctifying grace of God could develop the partial imbecile into the pure, simple-minded child of God, and even into the happy, powerful, and fruitful witness and ambassador for Christ. Dick's genuine character, and his true calling, became apparent in due time. What at first seemed to Mr. Henshaw to be a rude, indefinable mass, like a lump of ochreous matter from the metallic veins of Cornish hills, showed itself, by-and-bye, on a closer view, to be rich, high-priced ore adorned with its kindred crystals in their native forms and their original clearness. It would have been refreshing to see the Methodist superintendent, so evidently gifted with distinctive official wariness and reserve, carried, in spite of his propriety, into such naturalness of expression as to throw his arm around the redoubtable Dick, in acknowledgment of spiritual gifts and graces even in a fool.

The happy character and sacred effect of Richard's ministrations in the early Christmas morning prepared him and the people for other services and blessings. His narrative goes on to say:—

In the arternoon I praiched in Windmill Hill Chaapel, to a very laarge congregaashun.

Windmill Hill! What memories that name calls up! What a succession of hallowed geniuses and consecrated voices from the social depths Methodism had sent into the pulpit of Windmill Hill Chapel! No other ecclesiastical system, it may be, had ever given birth to a succession like it. There had been men of almost all varieties of origin, intellect, and expression. If the chronicles of that pulpit had been kept, two names at least might appear as typical marks on the page. There, that eccentric genius and distinguished preacher, Samuel Bradburn, used to sway the multitude with his alternations of thunder and pathos, and had left the memory of some of his wildest and some of his most happy and effective utterances. And there, now, came another thunderer, the "Foolish Dick," with a voice not so rich in its music as the voice that had passed; but, hallowed by "the same Spirit," it had like power to rouse the sleeper and wake the dead. It may be questioned, indeed, which voice, that of the orator or that of the "fool," gave the more lasting thrill and the more permanent blessing to the Methodist life of that old chapel on the Hill.

Among the fruits of the poor Cornishman's labour, one instance of conversion affords remarkable evidence of Divine sanction. Richard himself tells the tale.

Theere was a respectable man in Plymouth Dock who, the night afore Chres'-mas-day, dreamt that a foolish praicher from Cornwall was comin', an' that he was goin' to praich in Windmill Hill Chaapel, an' that he went an' heeard un, an' that he gove out a sartin text; then he waaked and towld hes wife ov ut. He went off to slaip agen, and dreamt the saame thing waunce moore. In the mornin' he heeard that the Cornish praicher was goin' to praich in Windmill Hill Chaapel sure 'nough. He cum to the chaapel; an' as he was cumin' in he looked up, and theere was the saame man that he dreamt about, and I was gevin' out the saame text,—"As Moses lifted up the serpent in the wilderness, even so must the Son of man be lifted up, that whosoever believeth in Him should not perish, but have eternal life."* The word cum to hes heart weth power—he cud'n resist ut. He gove hisself to Christ and to Hes people, an' es a happy and useful member of society to thes day.

The subsequent character and life of this convert were such as to make Dick's visit to Plymouth Dock a remarkable event in the Methodist history of that town. Nor did the spiritual child ever fail to prove his tender affection for his father in Christ.

* St. John iii. 14; 15.

CHAPTER V.

DICK'S ITINERANCY IN DEVONSHIRE.

IT might be fairly thought that distinctively Cornish as Richard was, in birth, training, temperament, and speech, his ministrations would be almost exclusively adapted to people of his own class or province, and that his usefulness as a preacher would, therefore, be chiefly confined to his native county. But, though he would be more quickly understood by his own race, and would find more speedy access to the sympathies and hearts of his native district; and though he was always sure of a welcome and of more or less of success in his own county; yet nowhere were his messages of salvation more impressive, nor anywhere more certain, deep, and lasting in their influence and results than in the Devonian provinces which he visited. The race he had to deal with was different to his own, less suddenly susceptible of Divine truth, less easily moved to think on sacred questions, especially by such styles of appeal as his; while, as more cautious, and, in some respects, more cultured hearers, they were naturally indisposed to bear with Dick's peculiar person and manner, so as "to give heed to the things" which he proclaimed. Nevertheless, the sacred energy and unction of his prayers and exhortations overcame every hindrance; and the songs of salvation which arose along his successful course from the new-born souls which God gave him, are echoed to this day from the hearts of many who have descended from the converted homes in which he was entertained.

Dick's own account breathes the cheerful spirit which made his Devonshire rambles so happy.

Aall thro' the time of my vesit to Plymouth Dock, the Lord gove me faavour in the sight of the praichers an' a plaace in the hearts of the people. Aw, 'twas bootiful, et was; aall was love an' harmony. At Stonehouse we had a love-faist—et was a love-faist sure 'nough; eleven sawls found paice in that waun mittin'. I praiched at Tarpoint, an' New Passage, an' Millbrook, an' Kingsand, an' Cawsand, an' Anthony, an' sever'l other plaaces 'round theere, an' the Lord was weth me everywheere. At thes heere time I had an invitaashun to spaik at Saltash, an' so the Plymouth Dock friends got a booat to put me up theere; an' when we wore cum to the land, theere was a laarge cumpany gethered. The mayor of the plaace gove us laive to praich in the 'ssembly-room, and gove orders to the constables that they shud keep the paice aall the time that we wore howldin' the sarvice.

In after years, one who had become happily familiar with the scenes on the bank of the Tamar, over which Richard had footed or boated it, found the savour of his name still fresh, and the memory of his simple, hearty, Christian character, hallowed labours, and sanctified humour cherished among many, many saintly people who had listened to his discourses, joined with him in prayer, and sung with him his favourite pilgrim songs. The fishermen of Kingsand and Cawsand had vied with Dick in warm outbursts of zeal and praise. The quietly devout souls of the little water-side retreat, Millbrook, had been quickened into unusual diligence by his burning words, and the choice knot of cultivated Christians at Saltash had their "perfect love" confirmed by the childlike example of the single-eyed "son of Thunder." Richard proceeds :—

From Plymouth Dock I vesited Plymouth

Circuit. Maaster Seckerson gove consent for me to praich in thear chaapel, which I ded; an' from theere I went ovver to Oasten, an' up to Down Thomas 'pon the hill; then out to Knacker's Knoll an' Tamerton, wheere they said that theere was a man took down under the praiching; an' they towld us that he faaled down like a quaarter o' poork faaling from off the huk. I went from thaise plaaces to Ivy Bridge, in the Ashburton Circuit; an' theere was Maaster Sherwell, an' he resaived me very kind, an' maade my coose plain aall thro' they paarts—to Brent, an' Buckfastleigh, an' Ashburton, and Modbury. Thro' aall thaise I went, prayin' an' praichin', an' gevin' the word of ex'ortaashun; an' the Lord watched ovver me for good, and gove power an' cumfert, and sawls for my hire too.

I traavelled to Bovey Tracy on that theere round, an' I was resaived theere by Maaster Hugh Collinder. I sleept theere waun night weth a local praicher, caaled Thomas Angel. When I was goin' up-stears to bed, says I to our deear kind hoast, "You nevver had such lodgers in your house afore, I reck'n."

"How," says he; "who have I got, then?"

"Why, doan't 'ee see," says I, "that you have got a faalen hanjull (angel) and a foolish praicher?"

"Iss," says he, weth a smile like, "an' so I have."

From Bovey Tracy I got back to Plymouth Dock; an' now I had to taake a lovin' laive of my deear friends of Plymouth Dock an' Plymouth. Aw, how they had bor' weth my waikness! how they looked to see what I waanted in a lovin' way like, and gove ut to me,—chaanges of raiment, an' mait an' drink; an' everything they cud do for my cumfert they ded, I'm sure. I ded pray weth aall my sawl on thear behaalf, an' have cummended 'em aall "to the Lord, and to the word of His grace." I was fo'ced to laive 'em and to turn hum'ards. I cum back to Luggan, arter bein' away from ut three months. Aw, I was thenkful when I found muther, and sester, and brothers aall well an' hearty. But the greatest blessin' was, that my dear brother John, while I had ben away, was convenced of sin, and was maade happy in God, an' had joined the people. Aw, "What shall I render unto the Lord for all His benefits towards me? I will take the cup of salvation, and call upon the name of the Lord."*

A conversation with Richard about his first visit to Devonshire is well remembered.

"Well, Uncle Richard, you enjoyed your visit to Plymouth Dock, and all the places in that neighbourhood?"

"Iss, I ded; sure 'nough; I've raison to sing, I have—

> 'All thanks be to God,
> Who scatters abroad
> Throughout every place,
> By the least of His servants the savour of grace.'"

* Ps. cxvi. 12, 13.

"I suppose you found a great difference in both people and things to what they are here about?"

"Deffernce! I b'lieve 'ee. 'Twas a deffernce, I can tell 'ee!"

"How did you get on among the bettermost folks when they entertained you?"

"Get on! Why bad 'nough fust. You do knaw, doan't 'ee, how they do live, like? Well, my deear maaster, 'twas some little time 'fore I cud gev up my owld way, you knaw. I was axed to denner waun plaace, and there wore a lot of grand people, you knaw. Well, fust they had fish for denner; an' what ded I do, but ait ut weth my fengers like I all'ays ded; an' when my boane was picked I flinged un ovver my showlder?"

"Did they notice it?"

"Iss, the laady caaled the sarvent an' towld her to pick un up from the caarpet, and take un away; an' so she ded. An' I thoft I must taake caare to do ut like that nevver no more while I was theere."

"I have been told, Uncle Richard, that while you were in Plymouth Dock, or Devonport, as it is now called, you took tea one evening with two old ladies, deaconesses of a Dissenting Church, who were very high in their notions in the predestinarian way; and that they tried to get you into an argument, supposing that they should be able to master you on the question. But I have been told that you silenced them at the first point. Is it true?"

"Iss, I reck'n."

"Well, how was it? Tell me what occurred."

"Well, maaster, 'twas like this heere. They axed me to tay, they two owld laadies; an' they wore laadies, nice-looking owld laadies, they wore. An' I went. An' while I was drenken' my tay, howldin' up my cup, like, 'tween the taable an' my mouth, waun looked ovver 'pon t'other, an' then says to me, says she, 'Maaster Hampton,' she caaled me maaster, tho' I 'spose she thoft I was a fool, and ded'n knaw nothen' 'bout thear doctren. 'Well,' says she, 'Maaster Hampton, do 'ee b'lieve that Christ died for all, do 'ee?' I knawed what she was drivin' at; an' so says I to 'em boath, gevin' ov 'em a look, aich of 'em, says I, 'I do raid, ma'am, that 'we see Jesus, who was made a little lower than the angels, for the suffering of death, crowned with glory and honour, that He, by the grace of God, should taste death for every *man*.'* So I do raid, an' I 'spose, ma'am, that ef anybody es left out, et must be the *wemmin!*"

"So that ended the argument, I dare say."

"Iss, et ded, I 'ssure 'ee."

There was a passage in Dick's life in connection with his visit to Dock, and touching the "wemmin kind," as he called them, which he does not men-

---

* Heb. ii. 9.

tion. It is a passage, however, which should not be lost. It is one which shows that Dick, with all his simplicity of aim and entireness of devotion to his Divine Master's work, was capable of that tender feeling without some experience of which a human character, whatever its other virtues may be, must be viewed as incomplete. A woman of Dock, or Devonport, a small shopkeeper, had cast her eyes on Dick as one to be desired as a husband. It was thought that whatever charm she might have found in his person, she conceived it possible to escape from the cares and toils of business, and to become the preacher's "helpmeet," so as to share in the easy living upon which Richard seemed so largely to flourish. It is alleged that an advance was made on her part. A finely-coloured Eastern silk handkerchief was offered as a tentative token. Dick accepted it, and was touched. The notion might have arisen in his mind that it would be a good thing to secure a comfortable home as the husband of a prosperous shopkeeper. The danger of this mutual disposition to harmonise love and expediency was seen, however, by Dick's friends, time enough for them to put him on his guard. A hint was enough for him. There was an end of the love passage. And when clear light fell upon the case, he triumphantly cried, "Our soul is escaped as a bird out of the snare; the snare is broken and we are escaped."*

* Ps. cxxiv. 7.

Not satisfied, however, with bare deliverance, he must needs vaunt his victory; and whether it was that the joy of freedom blinded him to the claims of women in general, or whether his infatuation with the silk handkerchief had so mystified him that he condemned all for the fault of one, he, in no gallant style, stigmatised the entire sex, by saying to a lady after his return to Cornwall, "Ef any wumman do cum arter me any moare, I'll set the dogs 'pon her." But though betrayed into this momentary warmth of feeling, he was not without moments of calm thought on the great question which had been pressed upon him. He could give reasons for his decision against marriage in his own case. His late nearness to the matrimonial condition had brought him seriously to think about it, and, in his way, to classify the arguments which decided him. It was not good for him to marry in this case, he thought: "1. Becaase I cean't keep a wife; 2. Becaase leberty es sweet; 3. Becaase she is better as she es."

Dick, however, was not an ascetic. He did not need the lessons which the Saviour gave to His disciples when His teaching on the law of marriage had so far failed to soften them that on little children being brought to Him they "rebuked those that brought them." Dick could make himself at nome with little ones, and be a child to save children. In this he was equal to what none can exemplify but those whose character is simplified by simple saving truth. So, when at one time he was enjoying the simple luxury of Cornish country life—bread and cream with treacle—and his eager indulgence had left such marks on his lips and cheeks that the children at the tea-table were amused at his appearance, he wiped his face with his bare hands, and then called off their attention by putting them through a kind of playful catechism.

"Can 'ee tell me wheere the fust seed was sawed?"

"No, caan't tell."

"Why, in the ground, to be sure!"

"Can 'ee spell thaise words, 'living mouse trap'?"

"Iss: l-i-v-i-n-g, living, m-o-u-s-e, mouse, t-r-a-p, trap; living mouse trap."

"No, no, my deears; that wean't do!"

"How do you spell the words, then, Uncle Richard?"

"Why, c-a-t, cat; that's the way to spell living mouse trap, to be sure!"

Dick had secured his object. The children clung around him, and he blessed them with good words. And then, as if he were touched with the plaintive feeling that he was a lone man, and had no joy in any little ones of his own, he rose from his seat, as if determined to catch that consolation, at least, which was peculiarly his own, and moving around the room, he sang—

F

> "I have no babes to hold me here;
> But children more securely dear
>   For mine I humbly claim,
> Better than daughters or than sons,
> Temples divine of living stones,
>   Inscribed with Jesu's name."

Dick's story of his life goes on:—

In the spreng of 1814 I stayed hum tell the laater end of May, an' then I went ovver to Porthleven an' stopped some time; an' from theere I went to Penzance, an' took anuther round thro' that circuit. My owld friends shawed thearselves very kind, an' wore glad 'nough to see me agen. In November that 'eer, I vesited the deear people in the Helstone Circuit waunce moare; an' arter goin' round from plaace to plaace tell spreng in 1815, I gove in agen to the friends ov Dock, and aall about theere, an' maade up my mind to haarken to thear eearnest invitaashuns. I waunce moare left hum for they circuits, an' on the fowrth ov April three of the deear owld friends cum to mit me at Anthony, an' broft me saafely to Plymouth Dock. When I was cum, aw the plaace was aaltered. Deear, lovin' Maaster Henshaw was depaarted, an' a deveshun (division) had took plaace about me, the poor Cornish praicher. This heere gove me great pain of mind, but I strawve to go foath, just as Divine Providence shud maake my way plain and cleear. I laaboured right thro' the circuit in every plaace but Morice Street Chaapel an' Tarpoint,— they wud'n haave me in they plaaces. Howsomever, the Lord wud haave me, an' He gove me leberty to spaik for Hes glory, an' theere was good done in the naame of the Lord.

Poor Dick was not without some conformity to apostolic trial as well as apostolic triumph. He, too, found that during a short passage of time there may be great changes for the worse in the spiritual condition of churches; and that when such changes come, he, like Jacob, may "behold the countenance" of those who were zealous friends once, that "behold, it is not towards him as before."* Dick's zeal was not more rude or less pure than in former days, but the ears of some congregations had grown more

* Gen. xxxi. 2.

polite, and their hearts had become less pure and simple, and therefore less ready to receive the truth from lips which, though touched and purged by holy altar fire, spoke "not in the words which man's wisdom teacheth, but which the Holy Ghost teacheth."* Or, perhaps, the spirit of Church order had come upon the influential few, and had taught them the creed that the Holy Ghost never works but in tune with authorised arrangements of human agency. However it might be, Uncle Richard's movements seemed to be too erratic for some of the Dock people, so that Methodist counsels in the town were divided as to this Cornish wanderer, and disunion among the hearers, in this as well as other instances, lessened the power and limited the effect of the preacher's word. Dick continues:—

From Dock I went to St. Germans, in the Liskeard Circuit, an' then aall 'round thro' Landrake, an' Saltash, an' Liskeard, an' sever'l other plaaces in that circuit. Arter laabourin' theere, I cum back to Dock, an' traavelled on to Tavistock. Maaster Jones gove laive theere for me to praich in the chaapel, an' the congregaashun was very laarge. I delevered my

* 1 Cor. ii. 13.

sawl, an' am cleear from the blood of thear sawls. Maaster Penrose took me into hes house an' traited me very kind. While I was theere, settin' down, a wumman cum in, aall at waunce, an' caaled out an' sed—"Wheere's the foolish praicher?"

I left her knaw wheere he was.

"Heere a es," says I; "what have 'ee got to say to he?"

I got up an' looked at her, and she was aall struck like, an' ded'n knaw simmin' wheere to look or how to spaik. She found her tongue at laast, an' says she—

"I'm very sorry," says she, "very sorry, I'm sure!" an' so she went her way, as ef she cud'n look at the foolish praicher wethout looking like a foolish wumman!

There would sometimes be a sudden springing forth of power from Dick's personal presence, which gave a strange surprise to those who came under its influence; a kind of glamour which unexpectedly produced a feeling of nearness to some secret force of command. Whether it came from his eye, or lip, or voice, or touch, or from all these in mystic combination, certain it is that the power was put forth on occasions against those who would fain despise the fool or trifle with him, and when it was put forth it proved far more than self-defensive. One instance comes vividly to one's memory just now. A boisterous, ill-tempered servant who, perhaps, did not like the task of paying attention to the poor seemingly witless guest, gave expression to her bad feeling in Dick's presence. Dick turned his eye on her, gave her shoulder a gentle touch, and with a voice something between a growl and a roar, cried, "Gloaryus Jinny!" Glorious Jinny changed her tone, and waited on him henceforth with great care. Something of this power was evidently felt by the rude Tavistock woman, who, as Dick said, could not look at the fool without looking foolish herself. It was Uncle Richard's mode of "Taming the Shrew."

Dick's evangelical rambles on the Devonshire side of the Tamar were now to be finished for a time. He closes his account of this round by saying—

From Tavistock I went an' praiched at the Canal Mine. My pulpet was the counthouse stears; an' the miners behaaved very daisent, an' shawed that they feelt the word. From theere I vesited Milton Abbot; an' while I was praiching, a lot ov wecked people cum weth braanches ov trees an' maade a wunderful desturbance. Some said, "The fool ed'n fet to lev!" others cried out, "Stoane un! stoane un!" At laast I cud staand ut no longer, an' was fo'ced to gev up an' run into a house for shilter. In the hevvening I cum back to Tavistock. My next plaace was Beer-Alston, wheere I took my staand under a great tree in the middle ov the town, an' theere I caaled 'pon the people to forsaake thear aivel ways, an' to turn to the Lord. From Beer-Alston I maade my way back to Tavistock, and then agen to Plymouth, praiching aall along 'pon the rooade; an' so I cum back hum, arter bein' away a matter of five months.

CHAPTER VI.

DICK'S PERAMBULATIONS AMONG HIS OWN KINDRED.

TRUE Christian piety regulates, while it spiritualises, the affections. It turns the heart towards the souls of men in their relation to Christ as saved or unregenerate sinners; and at the same time it teaches the heart to arrange the objects of its love in their proper circles. Christ first, in the centre, supreme, and every other according to its true lovableness, beneath Him, in its own subordinate place. And as is genuine piety, so is the zeal which it begets. Genuine zeal is well regulated and under order even in its greatest warmth. The zeal of some runs out after most distant objects, seeks the widest possible range, and the most foreign and changeful scenes of action. Home has little or no interest for them. The devotion of others is never away from home; and the centre of their home is self, upon which they spend their time and thought, their warmth and power. The outer world to them is a wilderness left to its own destiny. But pure zeal is under better rule. Like Andrew, who, in his first love, "*first* found his *own brother* Simon, and brought him to Jesus,"* it begins at home, and never loses its interest in those who are nearest to its heart; but, like the same apostle and his brethren, who " went everywhere, and the hand of the Lord was with them," † pure zeal takes the range of every circle of action which Providence opens to it. Its heart is always at home, while it is ever ready to go wherever it is called to dispense truth and grace.

Richard Hampton's purity of zeal was clearly shown in this true balance of his Christian benevolence. He was naturally an itinerant. To run errands had been his most suitable and effective mode of secular exercise; and his hallowed powers were now always seen to advantage in his circling movements as a pilgrim preacher. His favourite rounds, however, were among his more immediate neighbours in his own county. Always ready for more distant scenes of labour when his way to them was cleared before him, his heart at the same time was always beating for the salvation of his own tribe and class; while his deepest interest was in the spiritual welfare of his mother, his sister, and his brothers. It is instructive and refreshing to hear him, while recounting his toils afar off and the events of his wider travels, recurring again and

---

* St. John i. 41, 42.   † Acts viii. 4—11, 21.

again to the happy changes which took place in his own cottage home, as he believed, in answer to prayer on behalf of his own kindred. So, when he returns from his pilgrimage into Devon, he says—

When I got back hum, at the end of August, 1815, I found my bruther John goin' on in a steddy waalk weth God; an' by thes time my bruther William had united hisself weth the people. While I had ben away, he was broft to gev up hes heart to the Lord, an' was maade a partaaker of Divine faavour. "Bless the Lord, O my soul."

> "In Him, when brethren join,
>   And follow after peace,
> The fellowship Divine
>   He promises to bless;
> His choicest graces to bestow,
> Where two or three are met below."

I stayed hum, laabourin' in my awn neighbourhood, tell the spreng of 1816, when I staarted for the Truro Circuit, an' was well resaived at Probus. 'Pon a Sunday mornin' theere, the Lord gove me great leberty in prayer; an' while we wore wrastling, a sawl that had ben under conviction of sin was broft into leberty. 'Hes cup was full, sure 'nough, an' runnin' ovver. 'Twas a blessed time; an' the sound of ut went out an' caaled up such a feelin', that the Truro friends had a desire for me to cum theere. They waanted to knaw for thearselves how that the Lord cud aanswer prayer. They thrawed awpen the laarge chaapel, an' the people craamed into un an' lestened weth great attenshun; an' "the power of the Lord was present to heal."* Arter praiching in sever'l plaaces in Truro Circuit, I traamped away to St. Austell, an' keept on right thro' weth praiching an' prayer-mittin's in Roseland, an' St. Mawes, an' Gerrans, an' Phileigh, an' Veryan, an' Tregony, an' Grampound, an' Mevagissey, an' Charles Town, an' St. Blazey, an' St. Stephens. In thes journey the Lord gove me faavour weth the people, an' sawls for my rewaard. I was towld arterwards of

---

* St. Luke v. 17.

sever'l that wore convinced, in partic'lar at St. Stephens.

All these preaching and praying journeys were recorded in Richard's memory with remarkable certainty and minute distinctness. Persons, places, dates, were all marked and arranged with such order and accuracy that they were always ready for use, and could be brought out, seemingly, without any effort at recollection, on the most sudden and unexpected demand. He had been preaching one day in later life at Portreath, on the coast of his native parish, and was overtaken on his way up the valley by a gentleman who had been listening to him that morning. He remembered Dick's visit to the St. Austell Circuit in 1816, and now accosted him.

"How are you, Mr. Hampton?"

"How ar'ee?" said Dick with a responsive nod and sidelong glance.

"I have never seen you, Mr. Hampton, till to-day, since I heard you preach at St. Blazey, about twenty years ago, perhaps."

"Five-an'-twenty 'eers, cum fifteenth of March next," was the instant reply. In Richard's mental calendar each place visited seemed to stand precisely opposite to the date of the visit. In such particulars he never failed. He was, in fact, a living chronological authority to his neighbours.

His story is continued:—

From St. Austell Circuit I cum down to Probus, 'pon thear fais'en-day (feast-day), to help Maaster Haime; an' he praiched an' I praiched to the people that wore gethered to the faist. I thoft of Jesus theere, 'mong aall the braave doin's, an' thoft to myself, "What think ye, that He will not come to the feast?"* Iss, He ded cum to the faist; an' the people feelt that He was in Hes word, a Saviour still, at fais'en time now, just the saame as when He used to go up to Jerusalem, and haile the sawls that gethered 'round to heear Hes word from Hes awn blessed leps. Bless Hes Naame!

Who would not wish to have witnessed that scene at Probus Feast! Foolish Dick helping "Mad Haime" to alarm the consciences and break the hearts of a Cornish mob! To raise the thoughts of a frolicsome multitude from the jollities of a revel to the realities of the unseen world, the transactions of a future judgment, and the mysteries and blessings of the Cross!

* St. John xi. 56.

Charles Haime, by the intense energy and violent manner of his ministry, had gained for himself in some quarters the reputation of madness. His apology, however, was like that of St. Paul: "Knowing, therefore, the terror of the Lord, we persuade men; but we are made manifest unto God, and I trust also are made manifest in your consciences..... For whether we be beside ourselves, it is to God; or whether we be sober, it is for your cause. For the love of Christ constraineth us."* He had been one of the leading spirits in the work of what has been called "the great Revival" throughout Cornwall in the year 1814. And often had it been feared by his best friends that he would prematurely exhaust his life and fall a sacrifice to his own uncontrolled zeal and self-consuming passion for his work. His nearest friends had pleaded with him in vain for some relaxation from toil, or at least some regulation of his energies in public labour. Mrs. Haime, at length, requested a venerable leader of revered memory to speak persuasively to her husband, so as to prevent him, if possible, from shortening his days of usefulness. The request was fulfilled. As Haime was leaving the pulpit on one occasion after terrible exertion, the leader, of whose genuine zeal in the cause which was dear to his heart he could have no doubt, quietly put his hand on the preacher's arm, and

* 2 Cor. v. 11—14.

looking in his face, he said, with deep solemnity, "Brother Haime, do you know 'that your body is the temple of the Holy Ghost?'"* It was enough. The exhausted man felt the implied caution, and was from that time not less pure and warm in his passion for souls, but more reverent in his mode of bodily exercise.

This was the man who was now in companionship with the "foolish preacher" at Probus Parish Feast. The "madman" and the "fool" were side by side in the midst of the excited people, alternately thundering and persuading, pleading with God, and warning and inviting their fellow-men "to flee from the wrath to come."† Now Haime would be sending forth the pealing sentences of a sermon on "The wicked shall be turned into hell and all the nations that forget God;"‡ and now Hampton, in tones that held the multitude in wonder, proclaimed the Blessed One that was "lifted up that whosover believeth in Him should not perish, but have eternal life."§ Now Haime pleaded with God for the perishing people, until his exhausted voice sank into whispers of agony; and now Dick cried for the coming of the Holy Ghost, until his feeling of power with God carried him into lofty and thrilling utterances of jubilant praise. Both were mighty in prayer, for both lived in the habit of communion

---

* 1 Cor. vi. 19. † St. Luke iii. 7.
‡ Psalm ix. 17. § St. John iii. 14, 15.

with Heaven; both, as preachers, had "soul-converting power," for both were intent upon their object; both were unselfish in aim; both unreserved in devotion to their calling as evangelists.

Richard goes on with his story:—

From Probus Faist I went off to Wadebridge an' Camelford, an' laaboured from plaace to plaace aall thro' the Camelford Circuit, to laarge congregaashuns. But aw, I'm afeeard the moast ov 'em runned arter me from coorosity to see an' heear the "foolish praicher"; an' I doan't knaw ov much good that was done among 'em. I cum back in the laater paart of August.

I stayed hum, laabourin' in the word at vareyus plaaces in my awn neighbourhood, tell the spreng of 1817, when Cap'n Garland resaived a letter from Maaster G. Banwell, axing that I shud vesit our friends in the Stratton Circuit. My way was simmin' cleear afore me; an' on the fourteenth of May I left hum weth my sawl full of delight in the will ov my Hevvenly Maaster. Hes work appeear'd so gloaryus to me, an' I was so full ov thenkfulness for what the Lord had done for my family; for, sence I had been hum thes time, my bruther James cud'n howld out no longer, but gove up to the Sperrit's power, and thrawed hes heart awpen to God, an' cum waun weth Hes people. Gloary! gloary to Hes naame! Aall my family wore now in the way— muther, sester, an' aall my bruthers. Thes was a blessin' sure 'nough. Compaared weth thes, aw, what wore aall my thofts, an' prayers, and laabours abrooad! To cum an' find what the Lord was doin' for my hum. Aw, how shaal I shaw my graatitude?

> "My Saviour, how shall I proclaim?
> How pay the mighty debt I owe?
> Let all I have, and all I am,
> Ceaseless to all Thy glory show.
>
> "Too much to Thee I cannot give;
> Too much I cannot do for Thee;
> Let all Thy love, and all Thy grief,
> Graven on my heart for ever be."

When I cum to Wadebridge, theere was Maaster Titus Close waitin' for me; an' he took me, in a very kind way like, to Stratton, to Maaster Banwell's house; an' in that theere house I was traited as ef I was desarvin' to be noaticed—et maade me feel ashaamed, tho' my sawl was so happy. At laast I cud'n help no longer stricking up loud theere, 'longside ov God's deear sarvents:—

> "How do Thy mercies close me round!
>   For ever be Thy name adored;
> I blush in all things to abound:
>   The servant is above his Lord!
>
> "Inured to poverty and pain,
>   A suffering life my Master led:
> The Son of God, the son of man,
>   He had not where to lay His head.
>
> "But, lo, a place He hath prepared
>   For me, whom watchful angels keep;
> Yea, He Himself becomes my guard;
>   He smooths my bed and gives me sleep."

Next day was Sunday mornin', an' I praiched in a laarge baarn to as many people as cud be stuffed into un. In the hevvening the chaapel was ov no use at aall, the crowds cum flawin' in in such a way, so I was fo'ced to go up an' taake my plaace 'pon a hill that they caaled Stamford's Hill. Some boays an' maidens loffed a bit, an' behaaved unaisy, but moast of the people lestened in a searyus way, an' behaaved daisent, as they shud. Many of 'em wore struck, too, under the Word.

Stratton, the quaint little northernmost town of Cornwall, was, at the time of Dick's visit, the centre of a kind of home mission, giving promise of spiritual success. The mission had begun some years before, in a "day of small things," when for a time it might be asked, "By whom shall Jacob arise, for he is small."* The good work originated in one of the lowliest dwellings of the town, the cottage of a saintly pauper known as Mally Short. One who visited the town in later years as a missionary says, "Mally Short was the hostess of the home missionary, who used to come on his monthly visits from Launceston. Mally's cottage, mean as some would have thought it, became a centre of spiritual life. Once a month, at least, the little abode was by turns the preacher's study, and boarding-house, and lodging place, and preaching room. Whether Mally was a widow or otherwise, like her of Zarephath, she was ready to share her morsel with the prophet; yea, to

* Amos vii. 2.

honour him by offering him the better fare. She fed on barley bread herself, but always provided a wheaten loaf for the servant of God; and the purchase of such a loaf was the sure token to her neighbours that the missionary was at hand. Nor could she be content without a share in the honour of contributing towards the support of that cause which her heart had espoused; out of her weekly pittance the consecrated penny was always put aside on the shelf. That was holy, however she herself might fare. God honoured that woman. He created a " church in her house." The Blessed Spirit hallowed her cottage by making it the scene of many conversions; and within her humble apartment there sprang up the first fruits of that wide harvest which I have seen enriching so many homes both far and near. One of the best men I ever knew told me once that, as he knelt by Mally Short's dresser, when but a lad, he felt his heart softened at thoughts of the Saviour; and that as he wept and prayed, there came a sense of awe so mingled with the tenderest feeling towards God, that he was sure the Comforter had touched his soul, and left a divine impression that his Heavenly Father was pleased. In that cottage, too, the same lad, moved by the warmth of his 'first love' to Christ, very soon made his earliest effort to persuade his neighbours to be 'reconciled to God.' I should like to have heard that first sermon; doubtless it gave promise of the sweetness, spiritual wisdom, and discernment which so distinguished his ministry in riper years. He was soon banded with a few young kindred spirits in working out plans of usefulness. Their mode was to take walking tours among the neighbouring villages for the purpose of reading and praying with the secluded remnants of that scattered population; and in this way they did much to mark out the original pattern of that spiritual net-work which, under the name of Methodism, now spreads over so large a portion of that interesting district. Master Billy became a devoted minister of Christ; and after twenty-six years of unblemished reputation and ministerial usefulness, he came back a paralytic to give his latest energies to the work of a pastor in his native province and place of his birth; and the closing scenes of the truly Rev. William Hayman's ministerial life were scenes of rich spiritual joy and power."

This same William Hayman, while still a worshipper in Mally Short's cottage, aided by his fellow-converts and friendly neighbours, was the means of securing a larger place of worship in Stratton. Mally Short's cottage was no longer equal to the demands of the society and congregation. There must needs be a chapel; and at length that chapel was opened which Richard Hampton, when he came, found of "no use"—too small, in fact, for the crowd that came to hear the "Cornish Fool."

CHAPTER VII.

DICK'S LAST RAMBLE ON TAMAR SIDE.

THE chapel which Uncle Richard found so unequal to the accommodation of his audience in Stratton is worthy of a record —not for its size, for it was small, nor, indeed, for its architectural consistency, or its beauty of furniture, but for the circumstances of its first consecration as the refuge of the little Church which had sprung into life in the old pauper's cottage. So hostile was the general feeling towards the "little flock" that when it wanted more room, it was found impossible to persuade any landowner to grant them a plot on which to rear a house of prayer. At length two old houses in the principal street were advertised for sale. Master Billy Hayman was pushed forward by his friends to bid for the property at the sale. His offer was the highest, and he was acknowledged as the purchaser. Difficulties now began. He was not of age, and could not be supposed to give adequate security. But objections on that point were all overcome by his offer to advance the entire amount of purchase on the spot. No suspicion of his real object in this purchase seemed to be entertained as yet; and as some reason for the proceeding must be thought of, people got up a rumour that Master Billy Hayman was thinking of marriage, and was preparing a dwelling for himself and wife. Master Billy did not contradict the adopted opinion of the public, but, after the execution of the deed, proceeded to remove the floors and partitions of the houses, and very soon made it appear that a Methodist chapel was to be opened in the middle of the town. Now the public feeling rose to a storm. He was assailed on all sides, reasoned with, coaxed, flattered, and threatened. All in vain, however; the property was his, and he would consecrate it to a hallowed use. When all other modes of prevention had failed, he was summoned before the magistrates, with the design of frightening him into the admission that the provisions of the deed had been violated, or the property malappropriated. He proved himself to be in the right. And then the learned bench, foiled and vexed, declared that he must pay the legal expenses of the court, five shillings. Master Billy was not sure that they were making an illegal demand, and now found himself in an awkward position. "For," said he, "I had no money. In the confusion of the moment, however, I happened to put my hand into my pocket, and there were five shillings, neither more nor less. I had no money in my pocket when I went into court; and how the five shillings got there at the nick of time I never could find out to this day." The chapel was opened, and for some years it was the scene of happy worship, and a place of salvation to a succession of believing souls.

The "foolish preacher" found the Stratton public so changed from its former persecuting character, that crowds flocked to hear him—such crowds that the little sanctuary was too small, and Dick and his willing congregation mounted to the top of Stamford Hill. Stamford Hill was the proudest of old Stratton's sheltering heights. It was a storied spot. It had been consecrated as the death scene of brave men. The grass that adorned its slopes and rounded summits flourished over the remains of many a valiant troop, cut down in one of the fiercest of civil conflicts. The Parliamentary forces had once taken up defensive quarters on that hill, and Chudleigh and Stamford commanded the dreaded columns which had victoriously swept the country. But the resistless Berkely had pressed up the hill, on all sides against fire and steel; the position was carried, and the brave defenders fell in masses under the hands of the king's "Cornish boys." Stamford Hill had then indeed a baptism of blood. But now on the scene of fiercest strife, standing on the sod that covered the slain, there was a peaceful multitude listening with wonder and awe to a "Cornish boy" of other spirit and calling, a reputed fool, who proclaimed the "Judge of quick and dead;" and with a voice that might seem attuned to the final trumpet, was crying to the tremulous crowd, "Behold He cometh with clouds; and every eye shall see Him, and they also that pierced Him; and all kindreds of the earth shall wail because of Him. Even so, Amen."* The fool's voice that day on Stamford Hill was a voice of power, and the old venerated mound was newly hallowed as a scene of salvation and peace.

The two men who stood by Dick as he appealed to the people on the hill were somewhat remarkable men, each in his own way. Mr. Banwell, Dick's host, was a man of calm thoughtfulness and quiet humour, who modestly exercised his powers in the work of an unpretending Christian pastor. Titus Close was an evangelist in whose word there was much of "the soul-converting power." Among the families of that neighbourhood who shared the blessings of his ministry was one from which there arose the saintly woman who became his wife, subsequently was his partner in missionary toil and triumph in the East, and was the mother of the second Titus Close, whose ministerial usefulness has kept up the Christian honour of the family name. The two men were at this time happy in their united labours and accumulating success. Banwell had toiled for some time with no very cheering results. Close joined him, and then the joys of prosperity began to glad-

---

* Rev. i. 7.

den them. Banwell's humorous genius was exemplified in the first quarterly meeting of the Societies, at which he and his companion Titus Close united in expressions of praise for the fruit with which God had crowned their efforts. The meeting was held in the large kitchen of a farm-house. The people were closely seated waiting for the delivery of the text. Banwell was the preacher. And at length, with Titus Close at his side, he gave out with a half-waggish glance, first at Titus, and then around at the people, "We were troubled on every side; without were fightings, within were fears; nevertheless God, that comforteth those that are cast down, comforted us by the coming of Titus."* His quiet humour was felt by his simple-hearted hearers, and was then, as it often was, hallowed in securing fixed attention to the truth which he unfolded.

Such were the men with whom Dick now found himself in happy companionship. His story is given as from a glad heart.

From Stratton I took my rowt 'round the circuit. The people behaaved daisent, an' everywheere they shawed me great tenderness an' caare. When we cum to Holdsworthy, the sarvents ov Saatan thoft to hender me. Our friends theere had

---

* 2 Cor. vii. 5, 6.

hired a house for worshup, but the plaace was too strait for the people that gethered, an' thes made 'em look for laive to git into the market-house. They got laive, an' theere we went. They maade a soart ov staage for me to staand 'pon, an' very soon the plaace was full o' people. I took my staand 'pon the plaatform. Just afore me wore the few Methody perfessurs, who cud sing lusty; next to they, theere was a good behaaved congregaashun, an' at the fur end Saatan keept hes quaarters weth hes smaal paarty of willing sarvents—wecked boays moastly; an' they keept grizzlin' (grinning) an' yowlin' (howling) at waun another, an' at laast an owld sodger put 'em on to fight; an' then he took out a book an' beginned to raid to 'em, maakin' a gaame ov the poor "foolish praicher" like. They wore a braave coor (gang) sure 'nough, an' they ded thear best to keep up thear gammuts (sport); but, howsomever, the Word ov the Lord ded'n "return void,"—et was a word ov power, an' theere was good done. Weth me et was waun ov the best times in prayer. Aw, how my sawl was enlaarged, an' how my lips wore awpened! I had gloaryus leberty too, in spaikin' from they words,— "What must I do to be saved?"* The power of the Lord was among us saavin' sawls. In the coo'se of my traavels I cum to Kilkhampton. Theere was the plaace ov Maaster Hervey's "Meditaashuns," an' theere the Lord gove me sawls. Sever'l 'oined Society while I stopped.

It is interesting to learn from Richard's passing notice of the literary associations of Kilkhampton, that though he was "a man of one book," and owed the vigorous tone of his piety and his peculiar power of usefulness to daily communion with inspired truth, he was not without a knowledge of some other books, nor so void of taste as to be unequal to a feeling of interest in scenes hallowed by the memory of such men as Hervey. Dick could sympathise with what was cheerful and hopeful in the spirit of Hervey's piety; and could, perhaps, appreciate better than some more cultured readers the style in which

Acts xvi. 30.

the author of "Meditations" recorded his visit to Kilkhampton. "I have been," says he, "about twenty or twenty-six miles in Cornwall, and seen wondrous workmanship of the all-creating God, ragged rocks, roaring seas, frightful precipices, and dreadful steep hills. Oh, how safe are they who have so infinite and mighty a Being for their Guard! How happy are they who have so inexhaustibly rich a God for their portion!"

It was probably during his sojourn with his friend Paul Orchard, Esq., of Hartland Abbey, that Hervey became an occasional occupant of Aldercombe, in the parish of Kilkhampton, a mansion belonging to the Orchards. Aldercombe, "the valley of the alders, or elders, both native coppices on Tamar side," was an old quadrangular house, "with enclosed court and strong door, built during the troubles of the Stuart time." There, it may be, in one of the quiet lancet-windowed rooms, the God-father of the last of the Orchards wrote, in part at least, those well-known "Meditations" which have inspired so many souls with devotional pleasure, and which have given additional interest to the noble old church, whose fine Anglo-Saxon doorway still invites the steps of the pilgrim who loves to commune with God amidst the crumbling memorials of departed men.

One would like to have seen Dick Hampton in his musings "among the tombs," standing in wonderment before that altar-piece, supported on the one side by Moses decked with horns, and on the other by a starched-looking figure intended for Aaron, with cherubim above, and then turning to throw an inquisitive glance from his twisted eye upon the elaborate monument of Sir Bevel Granville, his little thick form waving to and fro, as if he felt that there must be something holy about the spot where Hervey had the thoughts and "Meditations" which had recommended themselves to his heart. Happy is the man, and good is the book whose memory and influence are all on the side of truth and love. To see Richard ruminating in Kilkhampton Church would be to have the thought excited that, while Hervey's name appeared still to shed a faint and somewhat melancholy light upon the venerable sanctuary, and the old house in the valley of alders, the character and teaching of Wesley had certainly left a deep and lasting impression upon the mind and heart of the neighbourhood; and if creeds are to be estimated by their practical results, there could be no mistake as to the side on which the advantage lay. Wesley never visited the spot until four years, at least, after Hervey had left it. "I rode to Mary Week," says he, "and preached on the side of a meadow, newly mown, to a deeply attentive people." "The next day," he adds, "I rode to Bideford, but did not reach it till after five, the hour appointed for my preaching." The apostolic wanderer must, on that day, have trotted past Kilkhampton Church, in which his former pupil had meditated, but the door of which was not now open to him. The zeal of his followers, however, had carried a spiritual leaven into many a nook and corner of the district; so that when "the foolish preacher" came, he found a people prepared to hear the truth even from lips so uncultured and rude as his.

Dick's ministry increased the number of those new-born souls whose spiritual worship gave a sanctity to the little rural Methodist chapel, more fresh and lively than that which lingered in the aisles where Hervey pursued his "Meditations among the Tombs." The savour of Dick's name and ministry still lived when Kilkhampton was visited some years after by one who says, "I found a strong religious feeling abroad. I came to the little unpretending chapel, and there was a crowd waiting to be admitted. When the moment came, I was borne along with the press, and scarcely felt the ground again till I was wedged up at the extreme end; and there of necessity I was during the entire service. It was deeply interesting to watch the eager intelligence of those faces all turned towards the preacher. And how the people sang! It was indeed the singing of those who understood their theme, and felt it too. My observation that evening, joined with the result of inquiry during my rambles, helped to fix an opinion which I had long cherished, that, when the truth is received with simplicity and heartiness, and the power of Christianity fairly touches the soul, the intellect will manifest a power of which it gave no former promise, will put forth faculties, whose existence had never been before suspected, and, in fact, unfold itself in a way to show that man's mental capacity is never entirely known until he becomes 'pure in heart.' Never did I see an instance in which the missionary agency of Methodism could claim a larger share in the blessedness of exalting human character, and of raising the standard of domestic and social virtue." This observer had before him some of the souls whose conversion was the fruit of Uncle Richard's ministry during his sojourn at Kilkhampton and the neighbourhood; and it appeared as if that power of fully developing the intellect so peculiar to the heart-renewing grace of the Blessed Spirit, which was so strikingly manifest in the case of Dick himself, was alike exemplified in those to whom his preaching had been applied by the Holy Ghost.

Dick could remember the order in which he visited the several spots around Kilkhampton, where, in the course of his pilgrimage, he bore testimony for his Divine Master, and left living evidence that God "made manifest the savour of his knowledge by him in every place;" that he was indeed "unto God a sweet savour of Christ, in them that are saved, and in them that perish. To the one the savour of death unto death, and to the other the savour of life unto life." And though he was ready to say, " and who is sufficient for these things ?" he could with consistency add, "we are not as many which corrupt the Word of God, but as of sincerity, but as of God, in the sight of God, speak we in Christ."* His account is—

Arter I had been to Stratton, an' Kilkhampton, an' Holsworthy, I veseted Cookbury, an' Thornbury, an' Pancrasweek, an' Shebbeer, an' Milton, an' Pyworthy, an' Morwenstow, an' Bradworthy, an' Hartland, an' Poundstock, an' Litson, an' Launcells. Then I got down to Camelford Circuit, to see my deear owld friends at Port Isaac. Aw, how they ded cum 'round poor Richard. They embraaced me weth affecshun, sure 'nough. I praiched an' prayed aall about theere weth great leberty. 'Pon my laivin' they deear people, I cum back hum in the laast week in August, 1817. I got hum weth a thenkful heart for aall the mercies that I had expearyanced, an' I found my deear owld muther, an' my sester an' bruthers aall clever (right) an' in good health, an' goin' foath weth joy in the ways of the Lord.

* 2 Cor. ii. 14—17.

This is Dick's last record of travel. Not that he ceased to travel. But, in the order of Providence, the hand that wrote at his dictation up to this period was to write no more. Notices of his later rambles, labours, and successes are to be gathered only from the living memory of his surviving friends, who still cherish fond recollections of the old periodical evangelist. Dick's sayings and doings from 1817 to the end of his career are matters of tradition. Tradition says nothing of him, however, but what is innocently amusing, or kind, or instructive, or good. There was always a curious interest about the strange little heavy shuffling pedestrian. He was generally found footing it when on his preaching rounds. He never courted companionship on his way, evidently preferring the quiet and uninterrupted opportunity for thought and devotion which was afforded during a lonely tramp. Nor was he less wary of trusting to any mode of transit but the use of his own feet, especially if those who offered him assistance were not well known.

"How are you, Mr. Hampton?" said a gentleman, as he pulled up his gig on overtaking Richard on the road. "You and I are going the same way; come, get up and ride."

"Raather waalk, I reck'n," was the reply, close upon a peculiar squinting glance of scrutiny.

"You know Mr. Berryman of Penzance, don't you?"

"Iss."

"Well, I am a friend of his; don't be afraid; come, get up."

"No, I shean't!"

The reply was final. The pilgrim would rather be alone and free.

It is remembered that a friend did prevail on him once to accept the offer of a ride. The friend, who was on horseback, rode up to him on his way to Penzance, and, alighting, insisted on Dick's taking the saddle; he was got into the seat and sent off. As he approached the town, however, not feeling himself at home, he managed to slide off to his feet, and the horse was left to shift for himself.

"Where is the horse?" inquired the master when he found Richard in the town.

"Doan't knaw," was the response; "I left un go hum. 'Spose he knawed the way?"

Dick preferred his own way, and would leave horses to take theirs.

But with all his oddities as a traveller, Richard never forgot the purpose of his journeys. He was always faithful to his heart's bent; and that bent was to do his Divine Master's will. While pursuing what he believed to be his calling, he was always to his time, and was never out of place. There was something beautiful in the regularity of his evangelising action, as well as in the quiet steadiness of his attachment to the people of his choice. Though to some, at first sight, his movements might appear to be erratic, they proved to be his best, his only mode of exercising his zeal, and exemplifying his love for the Church which had begotten him in Christ, with all the members of his father's household. It must be said, to Dick's honour, that through all the ecclesiastical agitations which disturbed some of the later years of his life he never swerved from his line of pursuit, but by word and deed ceaselessly showed how a loving heart can " keep the unity of the Spirit in the bond of peace."* He was never betrayed into argument. Silence was his refuge— silence and song. Once only he was heard to respond to a direct appeal; and the response was strikingly characteristic.

"What do you think of this stir among us, Richard; some of the folks are making a great ado, aren't they?"

" Iss; they do waant, every waun of 'em, a strong doase ov Bunyan's pills, an' a good pint of waarm repentance waaters to help 'em!"

The simple warmth, the modest courage, and the bold but regulated zeal of Dick's Christian character are consistently expressed in the last record of his experience, as dictated to Captain Thomas Garland in 1817.

My expearyance at thes time es, that I have laately found a grawin' in graace, an' have injoyed braave cumfert ov laate. I

* Eph. iv. 3.

have no end in view in goin' 'round, as I do, from plaace to plaace, but the gloary ov God an' the good ov sawls. In times paast, I cud'n help shaakin' an' trem'lin' when I used to see anybody cum that I thoft was cum to shaw a bad sperrit, or to loff an' grizzle, but the Lord have took away the feear ov man from me—I doan't knaw nothin' 'bout et now, I've ben a straanger to et ever sence, thank the Lord! I do love every Methody 'pon the faace ov the eaarth weth a partikler love, but saame time I do railly long an' desire that aall mankind shud be saaved. I shud like to be consedered a member ov society in Porthtowan class so long as I do live. I doan't waant to laabour in no circuit no further foath than is plaisin' to the praichers in that circuit; an' I do wish all'ays to be in subjecshun to they that are ovver the flock, as "they that must account." God es my wetness, I never looked to praich in laarge chaapels nuther; owld baarns staables, or any plaace like that; an' I b'lieve the Lord will shaw, in the day of account, how hes poor sarvent have tried to maake the best of the taalent that He gove me.

CHAPTER VIII.

RECOLLECTIONS OF DICK IN HIS LATER LIFE.

UNCLE RICHARD'S account of himself, as dictated to his old master, closes with the record of his return from Devonshire at the end of August, 1817. How long after this it was that Mr. Garland wrote the pages of the manuscript memoir is not known; it may be, it was not long before his "right hand forgot its cunning." Just ten years from the date of Dick's return from the last journey which is chronicled, the kind and saintly amanuensis closed his own mortal pilgrimage, and left his old pilgrim servant behind to continue his rounds, to pursue his labours, and to keep his own records; or so to live, and preach, and pray, as to fix a living record of his own later life in the fond memory and heart of his native province. The events of Uncle Richard's later course are recorded only by loving tradition. The memory of few men has been more kindly cherished by their own neighbours than that of Uncle Richard. Many a homely legend about him still floats around his birth-place, and lingers in homes which he used to visit. And many a soul that learnt to love him while he lived, loves his memory still, and likes to talk of his doings and to repeat his words.

One who knew Uncle Richard in his later life says: "About forty years ago I saw Dick Hampton for the first time. It was at Falmouth. We met under the hospitable roof of one who has since met his singular guest in the nearer presence of his Divine Master; one who, while here, was of the few who remember the Lord's words, and act upon them as if they believed them, 'When thou makest a dinner or a supper, call not thy friends, nor thy brethren, neither thy kinsmen, nor thy rich neighbours; lest they also bid thee again, and a recompense be made thee. But when thou makest a feast, call the poor, the maimed, the lame, the blind. And thou shalt be blessed; for they cannot recompense thee; for thou shalt be recompensed at the resurrection of the just.'* Dick was sitting at tea when I came in; and with his cup of tea held so as to rest at the point where his comfortable person swelled out from just below his chest, he was rocking and waving in his chair, seemingly in the rich enjoyment of his meal, and his social companionship. He was told who I was; and throwing a curious glance at me from his twisted eye, he cried—

* St. Luke xiv, 12—14.

"'Young Sam, es et? Gloaryus young Sam! Ar 'ee the son of your faather, ar 'ee? I knawed your faather 'fore you cud caal God your Faather! Aw, deear, how he cud praich! I do like to hear'n pray, too, I do! Larn to pray like he, my deear; an' the Lord will maake a praicher ov 'ee, too, I reck'n. Iss, "Instead of thy fathers shall be thy children."* Iss, "And Samuel among them that call upon His name."†

"That evening I heard Dick preach. He preached from his favourite text, 'And as Moses lifted up the serpent in the wilderness, even so must the Son of Man be lifted up; that whosoever believeth in Him should not perish, but have eternal life.'‡ It was the theme which from his lips had been so often hallowed to the salvation of those who heard him. He gave out the hymns in a way which showed him to be in the habit of 'speaking to himself in psalms, and hymns, and spiritual songs.' Like many, many a holy soul in his native province, the Bible and Hymn-book formed the bulk of his library. His prayer was close pleading with God; and I shall never forget the alternations of solemn awe, swelling desire, jubilant confidence, and impressions of power which seemed to come upon the prostrate crowd while he urged his plea. His voice in preaching had often a thrilling energy, though sometimes it was rough from being overstrained. Inspired passages, when quoted,

---

* Psalm xlv. 16.   † Psalm xcix. 6.   ‡ St. John iii. 14.

seemed to assert their own divinity and searching power, in spite of the provincial tones in which they issued from his lips. His manner was such as would, perhaps, render it difficult for some to look at him long without having their enjoyment of the truth interrupted or marred. The roll and wave of his thick, heavy little form; the awkward sway, now of one arm, now of the other, then of both, and the passes of his formidable hands; the grotesque shrugs responsive to the indescribable action of his mouth, and the comical peering glances of his eyes, seemingly in many different directions at the same moment; all in odd combination, gave to his deliverances what some would call a kind of weird power, which, but for the sacred unction which attended his ministrations, might have distracted rather than edified his audience.

"At the time of this visit to Falmouth the season was wet and winterly, and Dick seemed to be insufficiently defended against the weather. His gaiters were worn and porous; and we asked him to let us suit him with something better. He replied—

"'I was thenkin' that ef I had noo gaaters, I shud like to have leather wauns; they wud'n waant so much brooshen', an' I cud keep 'em clain better.'

"It was found impossible to fit him with a ready-made pair, his legs were so out of proportion, measuring but twelve inches from the knee to the ancle, but about eighteen inches round the calf. When a pair had been made for him, I undertook to button them on. As soon as one had been put on, Dick looked complacently upon the leathered limb and said—

"'That's clever, Maaster Sam! My deear, they waan't knaw me 'long the rooad, they wean't!'

"If any vanity had been indulged for a moment, it was soon crossed, for while taking the other gaiter from the table, an inkstand was overturned so as to throw a large spot of ink upon it.

"'Aw!' cried Richard, with a look of dismay; 'aw, that es a pity! Look theere! That es like a spot o' guilt 'pon a man's sawl; et spooils the whoal sperritjull man!'

"Richard was not, perhaps, without an occasional touch of vanity, careless as some thought him to be about his dress and appearance. Somebody had given him a watch; and I remember observing that when he sat with his friends he seemed careful to keep the chain and key hanging within sight, and appeared to take pleasure in playing with them between his finger and thumb. When he had been equipped in his leathern gaiters, a pair of warm gloves were also furnished. And he looked, now at his gaiters, and then at his covered hands, and there seemed to be a feeling something like what used to inspire primitive negotiators, when, like Abraham and the 'children of Heth,' they politely bandied compliments in the settlement of their bargains.

"'What is thear to pay?' asked Dick.

"'We will say nothing about that now, Uncle Richard. We will leave that to another time.'

"'No; but I shud like to knaw now, ef you plaise.'

"'Leave it all, Richard, till the resurrection of the just.'

"'I shean't have to pay for leather gaaters then, nor for gloves nuther,' was Dick's parting retort.

"Though he was never known to intrude his necessities on his friends, nor even to show a willingness to court their kindness, yet he availed himself of their benevolence in some cases with less of hesitancy than in others. He used in later life frequently to visit the little port of Portreath in his native parish. One of his friends there, who was a blacksmith, had observed that, from the peculiar shuffle and scrape of his feet in walking, there must necessarily be great wear and tear of the irons on his shoes, made some for him of extra hardness. 'In a fortnight,' said the friend, 'he was come to me again for new irons.' 'The laast you made for me,' said he, 'wore fust raate; they laasted a whoal fortnight!'

"Poor Dick! He could say, and he always said it with cheerfulness, 'I am a stranger with Thee, and a sojourner, as all my fathers were;'* yet his friend at Portreath had repeated proofs that it never could be said to him, as it had been to his predecessors in pilgrim life: 'Your clothes are not waxen old upon

---

* Psalm xxxix. 12.

you, and thy shoe is not waxen old upon thy foot, these forty years in the wilderness.'* With a worker in iron, however, as a ready friend, Dick had an equivalent with which he was content, and for which he was always devoutly thankful. And many a time would he toddle off with new irons on his shoes intoning, as none but Dick could intone, the promise, 'Thy shoes shall be iron and brass, and as thy days, so shall thy strength be.'† Or, rising into a more distinct tune, as he quickened his pace, he would sing a favourite verse:—

> A stranger in the world below,
>   I calmly sojourn here;
> Nor can its happiness or woe
>   Provoke my hope or fear:
> Its evils in a moment end,
>   Its joys as soon are past;
> But oh, the bliss to which I tend
>   Eternally shall last!'

"By the time Dick and I met again, his divination was fulfilled; and, as he said, I was now the son of my father in that, like him, I was now a preacher. It was on a quiet Sunday morning in the autumn of 1839 that I mounted one of the hills which overlook Redruth, and found my way down on the other side into the beautiful valley which winds onward to the sea at Portreath. The chapel, which was shadowed by the many-tinted foliage of the hill-side, just at the entrance of the wooded valley, took its name from

---

* Deut. xxix. 5.   † Deut. xxxiii. 25.

the old 'Bridge' that spanned the valley stream, a stream that was once as pure and gentle as the music which it gave to the woods as it passed on to the ocean, but is now troubled and turbid in its slavish subjection to pelf-seeking human art. As I entered the pulpit that morning, there was Dick in the official pew, or 'leader's seat,' among the elders, sitting and keeping up gently his habitual wavy motion. There was the distinctive squint of friendly recognition; and, by-and-bye, the unmistakable expression of his heart in full response to prayer, in happy unison with the music of hymns, in deep sympathy with the preacher, and in full enjoyment of the Word. There, too, seated near him, were Dick's brothers, in whose spiritual welfare he had taken so deep an interest. One of them conducted the fine, spirited congregational singing.

"The preacher's text that morning was, 'But whereunto shall I liken this generation? It is like unto children sitting in the markets and calling unto their fellows, and saying, We have piped unto you, and ye have not danced; we have mourned unto you, and ye have not lamented,'* &c.; and I shall never forget the peculiar manifestations of Richard's interest in one part of the sermon, in which allusion was made to the old Eastern custom of exciting mournful feelings at the burial of the dead by the

---

* St. Matt. xi. 16, 17.

use of the long funeral pipe, the plaintive and melancholy tones of which brought out the deeper wailings of bereaved friends; 'we have mourned to you and ye have not lamented.' Dick's appearance at the time was remarkable; some would call it grotesque. His face and form were all expression. Sometimes he seemed to be blowing the funeral pipe himself, and then he would appear ready to break into a wail at the sound of his own imaginary music. But his singular style of thought, his spiritual insight into some of the deeper meanings of inspired truth, and his joyous readiness to catch at any fresh illustration of his own 'one Book,' found rich expression in his prayer at the close of the service. The prayer was full of devout reflections on the theme of the sermon. The substance of the discourse was happily worked up into the form of appeals to God; and the preacher's appeals to the hearts and consciences of the people were finely turned into intercessions on their behalf. There was a gush and flow of short, thoughtful sentences. Then his soul seemed to rush upward and to gather powers of speech from the very throne to which he appealed. Indeed, the style, the diction, the stirring life, and the unction of the prayer were such as led one for a moment to think of Dick's origin, training, and appearance, and then to wonder whether what he now heard were really coming from Richard's mouth, or whether the utterances that fell on his ear were from some lips unseen.

"I was reminded of that prayer the other day, when a daughter of one of Dick's first kind masters, speaking of him, said, 'I hardly know which was the more remarkable, or which the more deeply impressed me in earlier life, Dick's strong and accurate memory, or his grace and gift of prayer. His memory often furnished us with amusement. If at any time he met my sisters and myself on the road, or anywhere on the farm, he used to give us his very peculiar salutation. He called out the name of each in succession, giving at the same time, without the slightest hesitancy, the hour, the day, the month, and the year of each one's birth, enlivening the chronicle of dates by giving little passing sketches of some circumstances distinctive of each birth time. It was on a rainy morning, or a sunshiny day, a calm night, or a stormy one. It was on a Sunday, or on such a week-day, with its calendar mark, if it had any, or its distinguishing relation to local events. But, after all, his grace and gift of prayer was the more wonderful. It was the more impressive from its hallowed character. It partook more of the divine. He was not always the same; but sometimes I used to be alternating between amazement and delight. His utterances really appeared to me to be like those of an old prophet in his ecstacy, when the power of the Spirit was full upon him. The paragraphs of concentrated wisdom, the passages of real power, the occasional grand swell of eloquence, might be thought to come from one of those who were in the way of the "rushing mighty wind," upon whom the "cloven tongues of fire sat," and who, therefore, "spoke with other tongues." Dick's language in prayer, for accuracy, richness, and force, and for its consistency with the inspired sentences with which it was so happily embellished, seemed at times to be so far above what he might be supposed capable of, that I used to listen as to something of higher origin; it was, in fact, a kind of inspiration.'

"The lady was correct. Her feelings under Dick's occasional prayers were akin to those of many, many who have found themselves brought closer to the Heavenly mercy seat by his reverent pleadings. He had, however, some favourite modes of expression, and some formulas of prayer, which he used so frequently that to this day they are familiar to many of his old friends. Often was he heard to finish his prayer by saying, 'Lord, look from heaven! Lord, hear from heaven! Lord, bless from heaven! Lord, save from heaven! Lord, take us to heaven, through Jesus Christ our Lord!'

"Several years passed between the hour of Dick's remarkable prayer at Bridge and the time of my next interview with him. It was, I think, in the course of 1843 that I saw him again during a short visit to Buryan, between Penzance and the Land's End. I had rambled over the bleak side and summit of Chapel-Carnbrea, and had lingered at its base for a little prayerful meditation by the old 'cross in the way,' and towards sunset came to my destination, anticipating the joy of an evening service in the village chapel. On coming to the door of the hospitable home, where there had been for many years a welcome for pilgrim preachers, I heard, as I entered, the well-known hum of Richard's under-song. There he was in the settle by the fire, rocking still, and still singing—

> 'How happy is the pilgrim's lot!
> How free from every anxious thought,
>   From worldly hope and fear!
> Confin'd to neither court nor cell,
> His soul disdains on earth to dwell;
>   He only sojourns here.
>
> 'No foot of land do I possess,
> No cottage in the wilderness;
>   A poor wayfaring man,
> I lodge awhile in tents below;
> Or gladly wander to and fro,
>   Till I my Canaan gain.'

"As he ended his song, he looked up with the same queer squint, now expressive of glad recognition, and cried—

"'Why, young Maaster Sam! waunce moare mit in the flesh! How ar 'ee? and how es your faather? es he able to praich still?'

"'Yes, Uncle Richard; and so are you, I hope.'

"'Iss; but I shud like to heear your faather praich agen from that passage: "There remaineth therefore a rest to the people of God."* I can rec'lect

---

* Heb. iv. 9.

I heard'n say waunce, how he had a draim, that he was in Falmouth Church settin', an' how Passun Hitchins cum out ov the desk to un an' axed un to praich, an' how he thoft he went up into the pulpet, an' gove out that theere text, an' how the paarts of the sarmon rawse up in hes mind, an' how he had such leberty in praichin' that he was waakt weth joy. An' then how he rec'lected aall the paarts of the sarmon when he cum to hisself. An' then what cumfert he found in praichin' that saame sarmon up an' down; an' how the Lord awned the word. Aw, that was a fine sarmon.'

"'Well, Uncle Richard,' said I, 'you must preach for me this evening.'

"'No, maaster, my deear; no, I cud'n praich; I'm goin' to heear you thes hevvening.'

"'Now, Uncle Richard, I must have you in the pulpit; you will preach, won't you?'

"'I caan't, my deear man. Ef you was'n heere, I cud spaik to the people: but I shean't taake your work. I shall heear you; an' I'll tell 'ee what you shall praich about.'

"'What's that?'

"'Why, that theere great long trumpat, an' that pretty little pipe. Sound 'em agen to-night! sound 'em agen! "We have piped to you, and ye have not danced; we have mourned to you, and ye have not lamented."'*

---

* St. Matt. xi. 17.

"Dick's memory had not failed; and like many of the people of his native province, he could easily recall the texts and even the sermons of those under whose ministry God had graciously touched his intellect or spoken comfortably to his heart. Dick remembered the discourse at Bridge; and wanted to have his impressions renewed. This, however, could not be by any means just then. It was too evident that it was far easier for Richard to repeat all the words which he had heard years ago, on that autumn Sunday morning, than it was for the preacher to recall even the thoughts which at that time he had tried to express. Dick was one of my congregation in Buryan Chapel. He took his place as usual in the official pew, 'the leader's seat.' He was sufficiently near for me to see how the flow and ebb of his feeling, during the service, swayed his outer man, and gave to his face its successive varieties of curious expression. Even his comparatively uncouth figure and heavily-featured face became eloquent mediums of expression to his evidently jubilant soul, while he was called by the preacher to reflect on the apostolic language of hope: 'Now is our salvation nearer than when we believed.'* His efforts to give out the sense he had of heaven's nearness reached their highest degree of intensity while his voice swelled into the triumphal tone of the hymn—

---

* Rom. xiii. 11.

'Nearer and nearer still,
  We to our country come;
To that celestial hill,
  The weary pilgrim's home,
The new Jerusalem above,
The seat of everlasting love.'

"Happy pilgrim! His brightening face and waving form seem to live before me now, as they appeared that night. My last impression of him was a happy one. I had worshipped for the last time on earth in companionship with 'Foolish Dick.' We never met again."

CHAPTER IX.

THE LAST DAYS OF DICK'S PILGRIMAGE.

IT is hard for some people, even Christian people, properly to free themselves from the old notions about consecrated places. Nearly eighteen centuries and a half have gone, and more than six thousand human generations have passed away from the world, since the Redeemer gave His great lesson on the question to the Samaritan woman. "Sir," said she, "I perceive that Thou art a prophet. Our fathers worshipped in this mountain, and ye say that in Jerusalem is the place where men ought to worship. Jesus saith unto her, Woman, believe me, the hour cometh when ye shall neither in this mountain, nor yet at Jerusalem, worship the Father. The hour cometh, and now is, when the true worshippers shall worship the Father in spirit and in truth; for the Father seeketh such to worship Him. God is a spirit, and they that worship Him must worship Him in spirit and in truth."* Yet still there are people who act as if they believed that to the living no place is sacred but such as may have come under the breath of priestly blessing; and that for the dead no ground is holy unless it has been paced by holy feet, or sprinkled by sacerdotal hands. Not that earth now is without her consecrated places. Many, many a spot has become sacred to human memory and dear to human hearts; not by mystic charms, or by virtue of ceremonial action, or utterance of official formulas, but as the scenes of Divine action, or as the places where the Redeemer keeps His purchased treasures. To put a human body which Christ claims into the earth is to consecrate that earth. That spot is holy on which a human spirit communes with its God; and if any action of a creature can hallow a place it is the action of walking with the Holy One. Many a retired nook has been so brightly visited from above as to constrain the lone pilgrim to cry out, unheard by any but his God, "How dreadful is this place! This is none other but the house of God, and this is the gate of heaven."† Nor can any spot be more deeply consecrated than that on which the Blessed Spirit first touches a poverty-stricken soul and quickens it into spiritual life; or where, by His holy and mysterious processes, He brings out the powers of an oppressed intellect into healthy freedom and appropriate exercise, by purifying and exalting

---

* St. John iv. 19—24.   † Gen. xxviii. 17.

the affections; or where the God of providence and grace raises human weakness from the dust, renews its energies, calls the renewed energies into unselfish activity, and makes that activity fruitful in the salvation of men " to the praise of His glory." On this principle it is that those who know what Richard Hampton had been, and have seen or heard what he became and what he accomplished under the government of the Divine Spirit, can never fail to look at the more marked scenes of his life as having a holy interest for all who " believe in the Holy Ghost" as the sanctifier of persons, and the only consecrater of places.

The point from which Uncle Richard sallied forth on his periodical preaching rounds among his nearer or more distant neighbours was not far from his birthplace—on a ridge of bleak hills whose broken seaward sides form the wild cliffs at whose base there is the ceaseless beat of the Atlantic. At the head of a dell which runs down to the wooded valley of Portreath, rich on one side with wood and copse and embroidered slopes of primroses, violets, and wild hyacinths, and gloriously adorned on the other with golden furze blossom, a clear bright stream running down by the roadside in the bottom, giving out its alternations of plaintive and merry music from beneath its continuous canopy of ash, and thorn, and oak, and willow, and luxuriant ferns, there stands the old thatched farmhouse of Little Nancekuke, its ivy and creeper-clad front and porch looking out upon a lawn-like field which stretches towards the high sheltering cliffs.

This was the residence of Mr. John Phillips, to whom Dick was obliged for an opportunity of exchanging his hard times at the stamps for the more leisurely occupation of farm labour. Here it was that he made his first and fruitless attempts at skilled labour. But these fields, and copses, and furzy commons were, as he said, the witnesses of his first happy meditations and successful prayers. And it was here, on the seaward heath, that he found his Saviour while earnestly praying in a wild hollow. The present venerable occupier of that picturesque old farmhouse has a lively recollection of Dick's peculiar appearance as a labourer, and of his odd ways of going about his work. And "I well remember," says the old lady of the house, "that when a child I was attracted by the peculiar tones that came from Dick's room, and peeping in at the half-open door, as I passed, I saw him sitting up in bed with his arms folded, and rocking to and fro to the music of his hymn."

On passing over the hill in the rear of Little Nancekuke, a furzy-sided path leads to the old farmplace called Cambridge, with its orchard and lines of elm trees forming a patch on the somewhat bare hill-side, of such a shape as to secure for it the local title of Cambridge Frying-pan. The quiet dwelling looks down through its garden foliage on a wild valley, through which a discoloured stream of mineral water rushes over a bed of quartz pebbles and metallic sand, babbling in tones which find responses from the distant rattle and thump of a rude stamping-mill, or the occasional cry of the sea-gull on his land excursion, or the cawing of the rooks on their way to cover. The trunk of an ash-tree and a rude plank, joined by an iron band, and held in their place by a chain fastened to a stump on the bank, formed the grotesque bridge which leads to the way up the bare wild common that swells in front of Cambridge—the first of a succession of rounded heights, here and there abruptly sinking into zigzag valleys, and rising one after another till overtopped by the bare carns that lift themselves so mightily, like unearthly guardians, as they circle around old Redruth.

Cambridge was the home of Dick's early friend and master, his " deear Cap'n Garland." And it was while coming and going from day to day in the presence of a free, wild, and open nature, that Dick's first inspirations came upon him. Here, amidst a remarkable mingling of the cultured and the rude, the wild and the beautiful, the bright and the solemn, the stirring and the calm, Dick first conceived the notion that to him the fields were not to be scenes of toil so much as retreats for meditation; and that his calling was not to work on the soil, but to call men to repentance; not to break sods, but to preach " the acceptable year of the Lord." And if any scenes could awaken thoughts about unseen realities, or the boundless future, and beget feelings of expansion and stirrings of spiritual power, they would be these varying scenes of Richard's errand-going life.

The traveller who turns his steps from Redruth northwards towards the coast, would find his way over a succession of boldly swelling hills, sometimes vocal with the noise of waters rushing from the mines, which penetrate their metal-bearing depths, and sometimes showing those "lines of confusion and stores of emptiness" which silently tell of exhausted veins, or of barren speculations, or fruitless toil. From every height his eye would command bare valleys, brightened here and there with stunted wood and furze-blossom, and running into one another around the spurs of the hills, as if they would mingle their vagrant, deeply-coloured streams before they passed into shadowy depths between the steeps which overlook their course to the sea. On reaching the top of a long upland road, after a pleasant peep now and then at a cosy cottage nestling in its garden, or amidst the outer sheds of its little farmstead, and passing over the summit of a bald ridge, just as the road declines towards the gully-like valley which winds to the sea between sombre headlands covered with the ruins of abandoned mine works, his eye would take in at a glance every point of interest in the scene of Dick's first and last period of life. There is the place of his birth and training, the sanctuary of his religious communion, the home to and from which he passed on his later evangelising tours, and the roof from under which his happy soul took its peaceful flight into rest. Just under the brow of the hill there are two buildings which stand as witnesses to the fruitfulness of Captain Thomas Garland's efforts to evangelise his Porth Towan neighbours. The more modern of the two is a neat chapel equal to the accommodation of the entire neighbourhood. It is a standing memorial of that deep and wide religious life which spread from a few pious Christian people, until it had hallowed and cheered nearly every cottage home of the hill-side and the valley. It stands overlooking the earlier sanctuary as if it would affectionately guard the little low-roofed, cottage-like birthplace of that warm zeal to which it owes its own loftier existence.

That more ancient house of prayer is still viewed by many with a reverence akin to that with which more ancient men once looked at the site of "the former house." Nor will the time be soon forgotten when the foundation of the "latter house" was laid. The scene might be a repetition of what was once witnessed upon another holy hill, when "They sang together by course in praising and giving thanks unto the Lord; because He is good, for His mercy endureth for ever toward Israel. And all the people shouted with a great shout when they praised the Lord, because the foundation of the house of the Lord was laid. But many of the priests and Levites, and chief of the fathers, who were ancient men, that had seen the first house, when the foundation of this house was laid before their eyes, wept with a loud voice; and many shouted aloud for joy; so that the people could not discern the noise of the shout of joy from the noise of the weeping of the people; for the people shouted with a loud shout, and the noise was heard afar off."*

Uncle Richard shared in this remarkable service. His voice was in the holy song, and in the jubilant shout. He had enjoyed communion with his brethren and pious neighbours in the dear old sanctuary, and now he had the joy of living to be a member of the greater congregation. He had seen the "day of small things" in his native Towan. He had marked the growth of the little society; and now he must take a part in raising the walls of that house in which he was to enjoy his last hours of communion with the militant Church. He would make another effort at manual labour, and have something to do, at least as a bearer of burdens. In attempting this he fell with his overturned barrow and crushed his left hand so as to lose one of his fingers. Thus he bore on his person to the end of his days the mark of his unskilful zeal, the proof that he could handle spiritual weapons better than he could carry material burdens. When recording his earlier experience he had said, "I shud like to be consedered a member of

* Ezra iii. 11—13.

Society in Porth Towan Class so long as I do live." His desire was fulfilled. Porth Towan Class was dear to him. It was associated with the memory of his "deear Cap'n" and leader, Mr. Garland. Many besides Dick, who took a part in the foundation work and service of the new chapel, had reason to look back with a feeling of deep interest to the beginning of things, the birth of that Porth Towan Class. The mother of one of the venerable men who shouted and wept as they looked at the old place and saw the first stone of the new one laid, was the first member of that fruitful Class.

Captain Garland, on his way to and fro from the mine, had conceived the notion that he might possibly gather some of the valley population into the fold of Christ; and overtaking one day an elderly woman, who was called by her neighbours Aunt Betty, or, in their style of abbreviation, A'n Betty Chegwin, he said to her—

"A'n Betty, ef I were to put on a class meeting here, would you join with me?"

"Aw, my deear Cap'n Garland," she replied, "ef you was to put on a class mittin' heere, 'twud be the salvaashun of my sawl!"

"Well, then, A'n Betty, try to get some others to come, and we will see whether we can find a place to meet in."

Here was a difficulty. But Mr. Garland's personal or official influence secured what then would scarcely have been gained by appeals to the religious principle or feeling of the people. Just around a bend of the road, as it rapidly declines towards the sea, there is still a row of low, antique, thatched cottages, sheltered by a few ash and orchard trees, with surroundings of thorn bushes. The middle cottage was the home of a man called Tom Tonkin. He agreed that the class should be formed in his room —not, perhaps, from any pious sympathy with class meetings, but to meet Captain Garland's wish. He proved, however, to be very whimsical. Now he would let them come in, and now he would shut his door against them. Aunt Betty Chegwin had been so far disposed to be good and to do good before Captain Garland had invited her to meet with him in class, that for some time past she had been in the habit of gathering a few children and young people together every week, in a sort of religious meeting, under a cherry-tree near Tom Tonkin's cottage. These young ones she called her "little flock." It was the knowledge of this, perhaps, that led Mr. Garland to propose to her the formation of a Society class. She pushed about now with fresh zeal to gain recruits. Her success was chiefly among the young; and several of these she persuaded to enrol themselves under Mr. Garland's leadership. They met weekly inside the cottage, when Tom Tonkin thought proper to allow it, and outside, under the cherry-tree, in case he did not. When the class meeting was held under the tree its members were often exposed to interruption from boys, and even men, who pelted the little assembly, sometimes with rotten eggs and sometimes with stones.

Under Captain Garland's leadership, Aunt Betty's Christian zeal became so pure and warm as to qualify her for training the young ones whom she had gathered into the fold. To secure for them the advantages of public religious service and the ministration of God's Word, she undertook to be their guide on all occasions to the village chapel at Bridge. And many a time has she gone before the "little flock" with her lantern at nightfall over the rough open road, two miles at least across the sea-side common. "And," says a lady of the neighbourhood, "I remember hearing my mother say that she was one of that little pilgrim company; that sometimes on their way they were overtaken by rain while going over the hill, and then their custom was to seek shelter under the bushes in a deep pit on the downs; and there, while waiting for the rain to pass, they often found consolation in singing—

> 'Praise ye the Lord! 'tis good to raise
> Your hearts and voices in His praise;
> His nature and His works invite
> To make this duty our delight.
>
> 'Sing to the Lord, exalt Him high,
> Who spreads His clouds along the sky;
> There He prepares the fruitful rain,
> Nor lets the drops descend in vain.'"

Very frequently would Aunt Betty stop on reaching the top of the hill overlooking Porth Towan, and stretching her hands towards heaven, would pray that God would graciously save the souls of her neighbours. And now and then her prayers have been heard to pass into a kind of prophetic praise, as she pictured the day when there should be a living Church in Porth Towan, blessing every home of that hill-side and valley with spiritual peace and joy. "Yes!" she would cry, "the mountains shall bring peace to the people, and the little hills, by righteousness. He shall judge the poor of the people, He shall save the children of the needy. They shall fear Thee as long as the sun and moon endure, throughout all generations."* Her prophetic vision was to be realised. Her "little flock" grew and spread out from under the friendly old cherry-tree. Other classes were formed, and from among the converts there arose a succession of leaders remarkable for their religious intelligence and spiritual wisdom and power. The first class passed, by-and-bye, from the care of Mr. Garland to that of James White; and from under the roof of Tom Tonkin to the happier home of Mary Nancarrow. The first little sanctuary was reared; and Aunt Betty Chegwin, before she passed away, saw the earnest of an answer to her many prayers. Her memory as a "mother in Israel" is balmy. Her son showed the influence of her example, instructions, and prayers, in his long life of piety

* Ps. lxxii. 3—5.

and usefulness as a leader in the Porth Towan Society. He, too, has passed away, with his contemporaries, the Hamptons, and other earlier members of that still living little church on the hill. They have gone up by scores from those Porth Towan houses of prayer to fill the ranks of the triumphant host. A devout descendant of one of the families who had lived to bless the neighbourhood, tells us that he can recount the last happy testimonies of upwards of a hundred consistent Christians who have departed in the course of thirty years, and whom he knew as the gracious fruit of the Blessed Spirit's work in the little congregation at Porth Towan.

Just below the two chapels, in the hollow of a field, on the other side of the road, there was the cottage in which Richard Hampton spent the last days of his life, with his sister and her children. Those children cherish the tenderest recollections of the old man and his happy companionship with their mother. "I used," said one of them, "to listen with delight, of an evening, as Uncle Richard and mother sat down by the fireside and sang hymn after hymn. Their favourite hymn was never forgotten—

> 'Away with our fears! The glad morning appears,
>   When an heir of salvation was born!
> From Jehovah I came, for His glory I am,
>   And to Him I with singing return.

* * * * * *

'With thanks I rejoice in Thy Fatherly choice
  Of my state and condition below;
If c⁶ parents I came who honour'd Thy name,
  'Twas Thy wisdom appointed it so.'

I remember how Richard's voice used to swell when they came to the verses—

'O the fathomless love that has deign'd to approve
  And prosper the work of my hands!
With my pastoral crook I went over the brook,
  And behold I am spread into bands!

'Who, I ask in amaze, hath begotten me these?
  And inquire from what quarter they came?
My full heart replies, they are born from the skies,
  And gives glory to God and the Lamb.'

I am sure Uncle Richard's last days were comforted by the thought that he had so many spiritual children up and down the country where he used to go his rounds."

That cottage home was for several years hallowed by its daily "service of song." "I shall never forget," says a friend, "how I used to go down, when a boy, to see Uncle Richard; and once, in particular, I was thrilled with a kind of solemn delight when Richard and his sister, as if the same devout thought had inspired them both at the same moment, struck up together, to one of our fine old swinging Methodist tunes, that glorious hymn—

'Glorious Saviour of my soul,
  I lift it up to Thee;
Thou hast made the sinner whole—
  Hast set the captive free!

> Thou my debt of death hast paid;
>   Thou hast raised me from my fall;
> Thou hast full atonement made:
>   My Saviour died for all.'

They sang the hymn through, and they sang as if the hymn and the music were coming from the depths of their souls. Though I was but a boy, I felt the power of their song; and shall always retain the impression made by the reposeful joy with which they sang especially the last verse—

> '' Yet Thy wrath I cannot fear,
>   Thou gentle, bleeding Lamb!
> By Thy judgment I am clear;
>   Heal'd by Thy stripes I am.
> Thou for me a curse wast made,
>   That I might in Thee be blest;
> Thou hast my full ransom paid,
>   And in Thy wounds I rest.'"

To and from that happy little cottage Richard went for several years, while he kept up his periodical preaching journeys. These were always according to plan. He never failed to appear at each place in its turn at the time appointed. Wherever he came, he diligently pursued his calling—preaching, praying, and exhorting saints and sinners to work out their "own salvation with fear and trembling." Everywhere he was welcome. He was supplied with food and clothing, and always had "where to lay his head." He was truly content with such things as he had. He asked for neither silver nor gold. No fare was too plain for him—no resting-place too homely. Always simple, always pure, always peaceful, he had the unbroken confidence of his friends; and never by word or action brought discredit upon his profession, or dishonour on the name and truth of his Divine Master. Many a time, to this day, in the different scenes of his pilgrimage, if the question be put: "Did you know Dick Hampton?" the frequent answer is, "Know Dick Hampton! yes, the dear old fellow, his quaint sayings and powerful prayers will long be remembered here."

The times between Dick's different journeys he spent at home, partly in reading, meditation, and communion with his God, partly in familiar visits to his near neighbours, or in manual labour, such as cutting furze or fire-wood for family use. Sometimes he would go down to the mines in the valley, still showing an interest in scenes which were familiar to him in earlier life. His only business at the mine was at the blacksmith's shop, to get new irons for his shoes, in preparation for the next round, or to have his furze-cutting tool sharpened. A good man who was at the mine when Dick used thus to visit it remembers how ready he still was to give smart retorts to those who were disposed to trifle with him, and with what penetrating force he would sometimes turn a passage from the Bible upon those who noticed him in mere playful condescension. One day he remained watching with apparent pleasure while they were setting a new engine to work. The leading engineer was present to direct and to see the successful result of his plans. They proceeded at length to fill the cistern, but all their efforts were vain. The water would not rise above a certain level. In fact, the cistern had not been made water-tight. The engineer had been passing jokes upon Dick, and had several times called out laughs against him. Dick kept silence. He abided his time. When the cistern failed, his time came. He looked on the parties engaged and laughed heartily; while, with a most significant cast of his squinting eye upon the engineer, he cried, "Aw, great inyuneear! 'hewed him a cistern, a broken cistern, that can hold no water!'"

By-and-by the time came when Richard's ability for travel began to fail. He had often said, when taking up his newly-sharpened tool at the smith's shop, "Now I shall drop my haw an' taake up the swoord waunce moore;" but at length it proved true that it was but "waunce moore." For nearly five years before his life's journey ended his movements were only in little circles around his cottage in the hollow. That cottage was his loved retreat, the scene of the daily readings, prayers, meditations, and songs which hallowed the last quiet years of his mortal pilgrimage. From that home he could command on one side a near view of his birthplace. It was on the slope of the opposite hill; a four-roomed thatched cottage it had been, surrounded by a few small fields and garden ground, sheltered from the sea by the high down behind it, the down on which there was the cave which he had dug in early life as his place for study and private devotion. On the other hand, the little chapel in which he had so long worshipped showed itself nestling under the loftier house which he had lived to see dedicated to his Divine Master's service. There was a turf-built bench outside the cottage, which was Richard's favourite resort when the season permitted. "Often," says a lady resident in the neighbourhood, "often have I seen him as, in my childhood, I used to pass up and down. He would be rocking in his usual way, and you might catch the intonations of the hymn with which he solaced himself."

A good woman who lived on the other side of the road gives her recollections too. "Many and many a time," she says, "have we, as children, got up early on a summer morning to look out for the dear old man. As early as four o'clock in the morning, and often at three, he was sure to be on his seat with his Bible and hymn-book on his knee; now reading, now rocking himself in meditation, and now singing, or murmuring his prayers."

"And sometimes," says another witness, "when the winter did not allow him to sit out of doors, I have, boy-like, crept up the garden to look in at him sitting before the fire with the two books of his library, Bible and hymns. Dear old fellow, he stuck to that cottage to the last. It was in a ruinous state, so much so that some feared it would fall upon him. His friends had left it for a new home, just above, on the hill, and opposite the chapel. But to him it was too dear to be forsaken. It had been his sanctuary, his home of filial intercourse with his Lord, and there he would abide and wait for his home from heaven. He was in the habit latterly of walking up to the new cottage to take his meals, and then returning to the old home to read, meditate, pray, and sleep."

In the course of four or five years before his departure, there was a gradual decay of physical strength, and a corresponding decline of mental power. Unable now to visit those who had sustained him as a pilgrim preacher, he was cared for by his friends and neighbours. Nor could anything more touchingly show the tender affection of those who knew him best, and the loving estimate of his character on the part of those to whose homes he had been so often welcomed, than the cheerful response from all who were appealed to on behalf of the broken-down itinerant. His warm friends, Captain and Mrs. Kite, whose prayerful and hospitable home overlooked Dick's cottage retreat, were among the foremost to help him. Mrs. Kite undertook to gather means for his support, and periodically to dispense the supplies.

His wants were very few. He had learnt Christian contentment. But little was required to supply his need, and to give him comfort in his last days. His need was supplied, and the comfort was given. And it was all the sweeter to him because all was done from love.

If anything seemed at times to disturb him, it was the thought that he might have long affliction, and thus give trouble to his friends and family. God spared him this trial. He enjoyed his food, and kept up his loved devotions, and shuffled to and fro, between his crumbling retreat and the new family cottage, until the 20th of April, 1858. On that day he said, "I shall go up waunce moore an' see Ann" (his niece).

"Our girl," says the niece, "came running in and said, 'Uncle Richard is out there leaning on his stick, and sleeping.'" The dear old man, like another, Jacob, had been worshipping "on the top of his staff," and, in his weakness, had sunk into slumber. He made another effort to cross the field towards his niece's cottage, but staggered and fell. He was taken up, brought in, and put to bed; and there, on the following morning, under that lowly canopy, in the cozy cottage chamber, and amidst those who loved him, he slept till his peaceful soul awoke to new life in the better land. His nephew was on his way back from one of the Continental mines, and it was hoped that he would see Uncle Richard before he departed. "Well," said Richard, "ef I doan't see un here, tell un to mit me on the other side o' Jordan—I shall be theere!" He was in thought and feeling a pilgrim to the last. His staff was dropped, he lay down to sleep, and rose up on "the other side of Jordan."

On the *third* day from that of his last sleep, according to the Cornish way of associating respect for the dead with faith in the Holy *Trinity*, Richard's friends, "devout men," carried his body to the burial in the churchyard of his native parish. He and his brothers lie side by side with their fathers, close to the tomb of his old master, Mr. J. Phillips, and near to the resting-place of his beloved captain and leader, Mr. Garland of Cambridge. No stone tells where Uncle Richard lies; but his dust awaits the resurrection beneath the green sod, overshadowed by an ash-tree, and sheltered by the sacred walls and the foliage of the upland graveyard, gloriously guarded, too, by the hills of his native province, which sweep grandly around the place of rest. To linger there, and think of "Foolish Dick," the quaint but faithful, the eccentric but happy and successful pilgrim preacher, Richard Hampton, is to have an impressive lesson on the fact that now, as well as in the apostles' days, it may appear that "God hath chosen the foolish things of the world to confound the wise; and God hath chosen the weak things of the world to confound the things that are mighty; and base things of the world, and things which are despised, hath God chosen, yea, and things which are not, to bring to nought things that are: that no flesh should glory in his presence. That, according as it is written, he that glorieth, let him glory in the Lord."*

* 1 Cor. i. 27—31.

THE END.

LONDON:
PRINTED BY JAS. TRUSCOTT AND SON,
Suffolk Lane, City.

Books recently Published
BY
HAUGHTON & CO.,
10, PATERNOSTER ROW.

Price 3s. 6d., Beautifully Bound.

HOMES OF OLD ENGLISH WRITERS.

By the Rev. S. W. CHRISTOPHERS,
Author of "Hymn Writers and their Hymns."

"A most interesting book, containing a variety of incidents in the lives of our great writers, with choice specimens of their writings."

"Having read the Rev. S. W. Christophers' former work on 'Hymn Writers and their Hymns' with considerable pleasure, we turned to this new volume, 'Homes of Old English Writers' (Haughton & Co.), expecting to find the same quiet method of imparting information that is not accessible to general readers; and we were not disappointed. He discourses in the happiest manner on some of our old favourites and their haunts. Those who want to know something about Latimer, and Donne, and Fuller, and Howe, and Flavel, should get this book. It is most enjoyable."—*Christian World.*

Fcap. 8vo., Price 2s., with Four Full Page Illustrations.

THE GLORY-LAND.

By J. P. HUTCHINSON,
Author of "Footmarks of Jesus," "The Singer in the Skies," etc.

Each Chapter commences and closes with an Original Poem. It is confidently felt that the book will be prized by all believers; while the perusal of it may lead the indifferent to decide regarding that future, which to them has been before but as a blank, and thus be the means of their entering upon the way that leads to the celestial beauties and supernal joys of the Glory-Land.

Price 6d.

PROTESTANT HYMNS AND SONGS FOR THE MILLION.

By BENJAMIN GOUGH.

"Well sung, Mr. Gough! Good, healthy rhymes are yours! Let the boys and girls learn by heart and sing them up and down the streets."—SPURGEON.

"Should be learned and sung in every Protestant household. The little book is rich with the glow of the grand old torch that was lit at Smithfield."—*Dorset Free Press.*

"There is much spirit with great felicity of expression."—
DR. CUMMING.

HAUGHTON & Co., 10, PATERNOSTER ROW.

NO SCHOOL LIBRARY COMPLETE WITHOUT

THE LIFE OF THE GREAT AFRICAN TRAVELLER, DR. LIVINGSTONE.

By J. McGilchrist. *Well bound and Illustrated, price 1s. 6d.*

"The appearance of this little work is very seasonable, and to young readers especially it will be very acceptable."—*North British Daily Mail.*

SCRIPTURAL VIEWS OF HEAVEN.

By the Rev. George Maunder. *Bound in cloth, price 1s. 6d.*

"This precious volume is designed to show what the oracles of God say upon our eternal future. There is poetry enough to charm the young, and plain truth sufficient to refresh hoary age."—*Wesleyan Methodist Magazine.*

By the same Author.

LIGHT FROM HEAVEN.

Handsomely bound, price 1s. 6d.

"The Bible and the Sabbath are the two topics discussed in this elegant little volume. To those who have not time or opportunity to read large treatises on these all-important subjects, we cordially commend Mr. Maunder's excellent book."—*Watchman.*

Now ready, price, Stitched, 1s.; Bound, 1s. 6d. and 2s.

GOD'S WAY OF ELECTING SOULS,

GLAD TIDINGS FOR EVERY ONE:

Or, the Harmony of Scripture on the Doctrine of Election to Eternal Life.

A VERY LARGE TYPE EDITION OF

A SAVIOUR FOR YOU!

By M. S. Haughton.

48 pages, price 3d., post-free for 3 stamps; or 4 copies, post-free, for 10d.

This Edition is designed for distribution amongst the Aged, Sick, and Infirm, and is also suitable for Reading Rooms, Hospitals, Workhouses, Penitentiaries, &c.

MAY BE HAD AT REDUCED PRICES FOR GRATUITOUS DISTRIBUTION.

Extract from a Letter received from the Author of "Hedley Vicars," "English Hearts and English Hands," &c., &c.

"I have long wished to tell you how deeply I value your publications, especially 'A SAVIOUR FOR YOU!' I hardly give away any of my own small ones now, I so greatly prefer yours. 'A SAVIOUR FOR YOU!' was given away largely by my father just before his precious lovely life ended in immortality."

HAUGHTON & Co., 10, Paternoster Row.

Stiff Paper Wrapper, price 3d.; Cloth, price 6d.

RAILWAY SIGNALS FOR LIFE'S JOURNEY.

In this earnestly written book "*dangers*" on the Road of Life are clearly pointed out, "*cautions*" are kindly given, and the Path of "*Safety*" made plain and strongly recommended. The writing is fresh, interesting, and thoroughly practical.

THE WESLEYAN METHODIST ITINERANCY.

By the Rev. Joseph Hall.

Being an Alphabetical Arrangement of all the Circuits in Great Britain, and showing at a glance the Ministers who have travelled in them from the commencement.

Price 3s. 6d., post free.

Such a book has long been wanted, and cannot fail to interest both Ministers and Laymen. It will also be useful to all persons interested in the growth and development of Methodism.

Price 1d. Monthly; the Volume complete, 1s. 6d.

PIONEER EXPERIENCES IN THE HOLY LIFE;

WITH EXPOSITORY CHAPTERS.

Edited by T. Bowman Stephenson, B.A.,
Hon. Director of the Children's Home.

"PIONEER EXPERIENCES" consist of personal testimonies by eminent Christians of Europe and America respecting the attainment of "The Higher Christian Life."

Thirtieth Thousand, price One Penny.

FREE SALVATION;
OR, GOD'S GIFT OF THE SAVIOUR.
By G. W. Haughton.

CONTENTS:—Salvation; what is it?—Salvation for you!—Salvation; how secured—Salvation; God's free gift—Salvation; its necessity—Salvation; its benefit and blessing—Concluding appeal.

"This little book contains in a few pages such a mine of precious gospel truth, that those who desire to win souls should seek to circulate it at home yet more extensively; and if translated into French, German, and Italian, would, by the Divine blessing, lead many in other lands to receive and value God's gift of a Saviour."—S. V. EDWARDS, B.A., *Author of "Jesus the Loving Saviour," &c.*

"I like your little book very much. It is simple and clear, and calculated to leave an impression for good on both mind and heart. I believe God will bless it."—Rev. F. WHITFIELD, *Author of "Voices from the Valley," &c.*

LARGE QUANTITIES AT REDUCED PRICES.

HAUGHTON & Co., 10, PATERNOSTER ROW.

Just Published, Beautifully Bound, Gilt Edges, Price 7s. 6d.

THE POETS OF METHODISM.

BY THE

REV. S. W. CHRISTOPHERS,

Author of "Hymn Writers and their Hymns," "Homes of Old English Writers," &c.

CONTENTS:—

Introductory Chapter—Fathers of Poets—The Epworth Singers—Others of the Epworth Singers—Two Brothers in Song—More about Songs from the Brothers—Other Psalms from the Brothers in Song—Clerical Song-Masters—More Clerical Song-Masters—Itinerant Minstrels—A Controversial Songster—Three Lay Singers—A Choir of Holy Women—Poetical Divines, Father and Son—Two Poetic Metaphysicians—Latter-Day Clerical Hymnists—A Poetical Satirist—The Tuneful Son of a Prophet—An Inspired Young Maiden—A Bard from the Mine—Three Poetic Voices from the West—A Kentish Lyric—Some of the Latest Sons of Song.

"In this volume we are made to pass, as it were, through a beautiful picture gallery of those who have, in many cases, bequeathed to the world some of the noblest hymns and sweetest poems in the English language.

"The productions of the sanctified genius of some of the Wesley family and their coadjutors are remarkable for true evangelical sentiment and sublime poetry.

"The volume before us abounds with proof of this statement, and is enlivened with a very large amount of illustrative narrative.

"Mr. Christophers has laid us under deep obligation for this most charming and able work."—*Living Waters.*

HAUGHTON & Co., 10, PATERNOSTER ROW.

www.ingramcontent.com/pod-product-compliance
Lightning Source LLC
LaVergne TN
LVHW061215060426
835507LV00016B/1945